MEDIA APPRECIATION FOR ARINDAM CHAUDHURI'S IDEAS, WORKSHOPS & SEMINARS

IIPMs youngest faculty member, whose claim to fame is that he's taken the Indian business world by storm... These top guys (CEOs & Presidents of the corporate world) – some of them his father's age – listen to him and come back for more. And Chaudhuri's USP ? His spanking new "Theory 'i' Management"... What makes Chaudhuri sell – and man, he does – is that he uses traditional symbols and motives to explain his theory... that is Arindam Chaudhuri for you. 29, a management guru... (**Cover Story, Sunday Magazine, Hindustan Times, 05-03-2000**)

Arindam Chaudhuri's Theory 'i' : Develop India centric management styles for managing Indians. Forget Ivy League, dig up home grown texts... Companies must do more for the poor... Chaudhuri questions the role of industry bodies like CII and FICCI in taking initiative in this regard. He points out that China attracts more FDI because their people have purchasing power... (**Cover Story, Economic Times, Delhi, 16-08-2000**)

BUSTING THE MBA MAFIA... Why don't we produce 2000 MBAs in each of the IIMs with such phenomenon facilities, acres of lands and huge buildings?... They (Professors of leading MBA institutes like IIMs) are comparable to our corrupt and illiterate politicians who don't want to educated the public... wanting education to be limited so that you can milk it... (**Times of India, Q&A, Edit Page, 14-01-2000**)

His "Theory 'i' Management" is now laced with quotes from the Bhagwat Gita... Going by the large number of CEOs and COOs that attend his seminars and workshops at hefty fees, it seems he has arrived... (Business India, 25-06-2001)

"NEAR – EVANGELICAL ACADEMIC"... As interest caught on and Prof. Chaudhuri went on to be known as a visionary, the workshops began to be exclusively restricted to the top brass... Prof. Chaudhuri addresses himself to CEOs and head honchos through his workshops because they are the ones who have their own lobbies with the CII and FICCI, which can in turn lobby with the government to bring about the necessary changes... (Business Barons, 31-01-2001)

Back to the roots... In each of his workshops, Chaudhuri discusses the American Management style and how it can't work in India... Indian management is like its economy – mixed... "But, we have picked up the wrong things", he says... (A&M, 15-08-1999)

Noted Management Guru, Prof. Arindam Chaudhuri says that purchasing power is the key to economic growth... economic prosperity for a nation is not about economics alone. For, a nation cannot be run like a department store... Chaudhuri's iconoclastic "Theory 'i' Management" is all about India friendly management styles for Indian corporates... (The Indian Express, Mumbai, 19-11-2000)

When Economist and Management Guru Arindam Chaudhuri talks on management issues Chief Executives pay around Rs. 25,000/- each to listen. His management philosophy for corporate

restructuring involves enhancing the legal system...
(Business Standard, 05-12-2000)

Indian Guru chants new management mantra...
Chaudhuri has developed "Theory 'i' Management"
a management solution typical for the Indian
corporate problems... while providing consultancy
and addressing the problems of the Indian
corporate sector, he developed this theory...
(Telegraph, 15-04-2001)

**An economy guided completely by market
forces lacks in human values** and is not suitable
for India... leading economist (Arindam Chaudhuri)
said here... saying that the market system was a
good servant but a bad master, he added, "There
is something animalistic about the survival of the
fittest paradigm. I would rather opt for survival of
the weakest philosophy."... (Hindu Business Line,
15-07-1999)

**Motivator Arindam Chaudhuri helps top level
corporate managers** raise their level of
preparedness to meet global business challenges...
(The Financial Express, 13-06-1999).

THE EPIC MANAGEMENT... Theory 'i'
Management advocates that old management
stereotypes should give ways more pragmatic
approaches... (Pioneer, 25-09-2000)

What makes this management guru tick? Or
what makes the Indian CEOs, Presidents and
Directors shell out Rs. 25,000/- for a mere six hour
workshop session?... He is only 29... Suave,
Articulate and specializes in Strategic Vision,
Leadership and Social Sector Consulting... (**The
Free Press Journal, 20-11-2000**)

Management School **TIME**, has awarded Prof. Arindam Chaudhuri the **Management Guru 2000 award,** for his extensive and remarkable work in the area of imparting management education and serving one of the top business management institute in India... **(Hindustan Times, 21-12-200)**

His irreverence would get to you. But so would the cold facts he logically presents. The list of observations is unending. "India is a sleepy cow" being just one... Mr. Chaudhuri's Great Indian Dream would probably give the government, economists, the administrative machinery and even tax payers sleepless nights. But his audience seem to actually carry home some faith in what he strongly recommended on Friday evening... **(Times of India, Mumbai, 03-10-2000)**

He has trained close to 3000 managers in it ("Theory 'i' Management") and now entire organizations want to adapt it... The next step in his theory is to tackle the Great Indian Dream... **(Business India, 01-05-2000)**

Meet Arindam Chaudhuri... Management guru with a difference. Here is a man with a vision... trying to strike a balance between dreams and a vision - "The Great Indian Dream" that he terms it as. (Times of India, Delhi Times, 05-04-2001)

If you think you can, you are right... Chaudhuri says, a good leader is one who searches for challenging opportunities and experiments to take risks and learn from mistakes. He gave a new analysis of leadership, in which the importance is given to the person whom the leader is leading... (Hindustan Times, Cover Story, HT Careers, 01-07-1999)

Idol to Ideal... "His (Lord Krishna's) actions and the Bhagwad Gita hold extensive lessons for modern Indian managers" avers Chaudhuri, the management guru... The crux of his theory is that what might be a flourishing management practice in a given situation might end up as a complete failure in another situation... **(Times of India, Cover Story, Education Times, Delhi, 11-09-2000)**

Leadership tailored to the psyche. Western management theories are not suited to the unique Indian psychology, professed management guru Arindam Chaudhuri... Through various examples, cases & lively anecdotes, he facilitated the rediscovery of Lord Krishna as the ideal leader in the Indian context... The five hour workshop was attended by over 35 corporate heads of India... **(Hindustan Times, 14-06-2001)**

The Mahabharatha and the Gita could soon be an inspiration for many managers and businessmen. Prof. Arindam Chaudhuri... has picked up threads from these two epics and built the leadership success multiplier model of "Theory 'i' Management"... **(Financial Express, 15-04-2001)**

Under the helm of **a trail blazer**... Several seminars have been held by Prof. Arindam Chaudhuri in which he has highlighted eye opening facts – which are a result of their (IIPM's) in-house research... **(Pioneer, 19-06-2000)**

Managing People: an international perspective. In the seminar management expert Arindam Chaudhuri enthralled the audience not only by his expertise in talking on management matters but also by his wit and humour... **(Times of India, New Delhi, 02-07-2001)**

GURU COOL... You thought a man in a ponytail doesn't look like a corporate guru ? See Arindam Chaudhuri and you will change your mind. This Bengali young man was in Calcutta recently to conduct a seminar "The Great Indian Dream"... **(Cover Story, HT City, Calcutta, 29-05-2000)**

Clinton, Clinton, Clinton Sang the entire nation... Nevertheless... Chaudhuri spoke on the Great Indian Dream at a seminar organized by Planman recently where he reiterated his call for the last days of American Supremacy from a socio economic perspective... (he) felt that capitalism today needs re-engineering and restructuring so that the social face emerges... **(Times of India, Delhi, 24-04-2000)**

"Don't imitate the free market system blindly" he (Arindam Chaudhuri) warns... in a country of about 900 million people, a whole lot of economic activity is taking place targeting just 30 to 40 million people... **(ET Interactive, Economic Times, 11-08-1999)**

Economist flays brain drain, suggests adoption of Japan, China example. **Noted economist and Motivational Guru Arindam Chaudhuri hit out at the trend among many young Indians to hate** for the US to become NRIs... "Compulsory primary education laws must be enacted and strictly enforced... because society gains more from an educated man than for an uneducated person," he said... **(Times of India, Delhi, 29-03-2000)**

He has been invited for numerous television shows including Budget day analysis on STAR NEWS & ZEE NEWS and celebrity shows like MOVERS & SHAKERS. Currently, he has a weekly column with HINDUSTAN TIMES wherein he analyses companies from corporate India.

COUNT YOUR Chickens BEFORE THEY HATCH

ARINDAM CHAUDHURI

VIKAS PUBLISHING HOUSE PVT LTD

VIKAS PUBLISHING HOUSE PVT LTD

576, Masjid Road, Jangpura, **New Delhi**-110 014
Phones: 4314605, 4315313 • Fax: 91-11-4310879
E-mail: *orders@vikas.gobookshopping.com*
Internet: *www.vikaseforum.com*

First Floor, N.S. Bhawan, 4th Cross, 4th Main,
Gandhi Nagar, **Bangalore**-560 009 • Phone : 2204639

F-20, Nand Dham Industrial Estate, Marol,
Andheri (East), **Mumbai**-400 059 • Phone : 8502333, 8502324

35, Palm Avenue, **Kolkata**-700 019 • Phone : 2872575

A-26, 4th floor, Nelson Chambers, Nelson Manickam Road,
Aminjikarai, **Chennai**-600 029

Distributors:
UBS PUBLISHERS' DISTRIBUTORS LTD

5, Ansari Road, **New Delhi**-110 002
Ph. 3273601, 3266646 • Fax : 3276593, 3274261
E-mail: *orders@gobookshopping.com* • Internet: *www.gobookshopping.com*
• 10, First Main Road, Gandhi Nagar, **Bangalore**-560 009 • Ph. 2263901
• 6, Sivaganga Road, Nungambakkam, **Chennai**-600 034 • Ph. 8276355
• 8/1-B, Chowringhee Lane, **Kolkata**-700 016 • Ph. 2441821, 2442910
• 5-A, Rajendra Nagar, **Patna**- 800 016 • Ph. 672856, 656169
• 80, Noronha Road, Cantonment, **Kanpur**-208 004 • Ph. 369124, 362665

Distributors for Western India:
PREFACE BOOKS

223, Cama Industrial Estate, 2nd Floor,
Sun Mill Compound, Lower Parel (W), **Mumbai**-400 013

First Published 2001
Copyright © 2001, Author

The book was developed, edited and produced at:

Vijay Nicole Imprints

Consultant Publisher : P K Madhavan
Project Coordinator : Pradeep Kumar
Editorial Team : R Dheeba, MS Chitra

A-25, 4th Floor, Nelson Chambers,
115, Nelson Manickam Road,
Aminjikarai, Chennai - 600 029
Ph: 374 3062 / 374 1084
Email : pkmadhu@md3.vsnl.net.in

Information contained in this book has been published by VIKAS Publishing House Pvt.
Ltd. and has been obtained by its authors from sources believed to be reliable and are
correct to the best of their knowledge. However, the publisher and its authors shall in no
event be liable for any errors, omissions or damages arising out of use of this information
and specifically disclaim any implied warranties or merchantability or fitness for any
particular use.

Typeset by Windom Publishing Pvt Ltd, Chennai
Printed at Modern Printers, Delhi-110 032

To my mother,
whose love and silent support enriches my life.
Her parents named her Ratna,
which in Bengali means 'Gem',
and all those who know her would swear
that she has more than
lived upto their expectations.

The Making of
Count your chickens
before they hatch
(CYCBTH)

Man proposes, God disposes.

Yet, man achieves... Often against all odds. Some men (and at times women too*) keep on achieving. This book will talk about them and about how to become like them. Thus, it will talk about "counting your chickens before they hatch".

I am not a motivation guru. After completing my business studies, I was bitten by the consulting bug. Mainly, I was influenced by the exceptional faculty who taught me at Indian Institute of Planning and Management (IIPM). While teaching they would keep referring to their consulting assignments... and that should explain it all. I started *Planman Consulting*, in 1996 June and, finally I can reveal - I was all of 24 years and 6 months then. When you enter a profession of grey haired people at that age you need to have something unique up your sleeves. At IIPM, Dr. N.R.Chatterjee and Dr. M.K.Chaudhuri had given me exactly that. Exceptionally original that Prof. Chatterjee was, he taught us to look at management from

---

* this one obviously is a joke. Wherever I have written man/he in this book, it applies to both the sexes, as it generally happens.

an India-centric point of view. To add weight to this outlook were equally bold and original ideas of Prof. Chaudhuri, who made our understanding of economics absolutely radical with his analysis of planned national economies like USSR & China. His ideas on how to make the Indian legal system (which is practically almost defunct) work and the importance of an effective legal system for a country's success made a big impact. Thus, *Theory 'i' Management"*, knowledge gained at IIPM, was put in the form of a theory after careful integration, industry interactions and detailed research.

Left to me, this would have been a book only on "Theory 'i' Management" because that's what I am most passionate about. My friends and advisors Amit Saxena, Shikha & others told me to include the rest of the chapters as well and make it a comprehensive book on success. They felt that the way our organisation is managed and the thoughts on managing people that I believed in would also add up to make the book more readable and interesting. Thus, this book has three distinctly different flavours merging with each other from time to time. At one time I talk about my personal experiences and it sounds autobiographical... at another time I talk about values and skills I believe in and have worked hard to inculcate, and at yet another time I talk of theories and research findings (being an academic myself, I can't help myself referring to theories*). I hope the blend adds value.

If it doesn't, then, Naveen Chamoli and Subho Shekhar Bhattacharjee (the key trainers and consultants at *Planman*)

---

* Being based on personal experiences and our research findings the bibliography became superfluous. I have tried my best to quote the references in the text itself.

would have to share the blame... they helped me out extensively with the second and third chapters. And in such a case, I hope Dr. J.K.Mitra and Prof. S.Kaimal (on whose teachings these two chapters are inspired) would be as angry with them as on me.

For the creative layout, the patience of typing all this while I dictated (often with breaks of one hour between two words) and all the spelling mistakes, I must thank Shishir Bhattacharjee. While writing this book I realised that his creativity is something that is so often taken for granted.

Every bit adds value... The passion and love with which my colleague Rohit convinced me to pose for a photo session (Rohit is extremely passionate about his hobby of photography) resulted into the cover picture being taken. People tell me that this photograph will add to my success in the long run. I try to use it wherever required!

Thanks are due to all my teachers, friends and the countless number of well wishers whose guidance and support keeps me going. I can't name them all but I sincerely thank them. In particular, Poonam Goel of *Hindustan Times* and Shalini Singh of *Economic Times* inspired me by putting their faith in my thoughts... I am sure Poonam would be finally pleased to see the book in reality!

All my workshop and seminar participants (who are seduced, and at times forced to attend my workshops, thanks to Arnab's exceptional marketing and stalking skills) have inspired me by putting their faith in me, thanks are due to them as well... in particular to Mr. Pankaj Munjal and Mr. Vasant Sathe who have constantly been a source of motivation.

I am also grateful to endless number of successful people, legends in their own right (living or not) for leading their lives in a manner that inspires me and millions of others. Dale Carnegie was exceptional. Hersey & Blanchard's analysis of situational leadership is one of the most original works (assuming that they did not flick some stuff from the Bhagwad Gita) I have ever read. Jack Canfield and Jacqueline Miller's "Heart At Work" should be read by all those who do not find meaning in life and Malcom Kushner's "The Light Touch' by all those who are not gifted enough to understand the importance of humour in life. They are the guiding force behind "CYCBTH".

Writing a book can be a tough job specially if its at the cost of work. Thankfully, at *Planman* I have wonderful people taking care of my bread and butter. Deepak, Nitin and Rahul see to it that my most important branch in Mumbai operates smoothly and I can concentrate on things I love (to watch movies, play cricket & write) without worrying! All others in my various other branches are no less and I must say their love for me and *Planman* keeps me going.

I guess some of you may not have actually bought this book (or may be many more would have??) if it were titled 'The Kamasutra of Success' (as Abhimanyu suggested) or 'Ditch the Bitch called Failure' (as Rajat suggested). Yet their contributions during the brain storming sessions can't be written off, since, it tested Prashanto's creativity to the hilt and made him come up with the awesome title of CYCBTH (awesome because I liked it very much) for this book. Though I am not very impressed with stray dogs, yet (for coming up with the name of the book) as promised I will put 5%

of all the earnings for the cause of stray dogs and animals which Prashanto is so passionate about. The rest will go to the "Great Indian Dream Foundation" which we set up in memory of my brother Aurobindo, to carry on social development projects.

When I first started looking out for publishers, I was shocked to learn about the poor state of the Indian publishing industry. I had grown up reading books which sold more than a million copies, hearing of million dollar advances... and here the publishers were telling me that books make to the best seller list often selling a meagre 1500 to 2000 copies! Based on these forecasts they offer cheap royalties and demeaning advances (which go upto Rs.15000). I decided that if a publisher believed that my book would sell 1500 copies, I would rather not go ahead with him and go about publishing it myself. That's when I met the young and wonderful Piyush, an MBA and the Director of Vikas Publishing. We struck a rapport instantly. His enthusiasm is contagious... His offer was irresistible. The amount and the royalty was important for me not because of the money but to know that my publisher believes in me. My first chapter will tell you that beliefs do wonders. That's exactly what it did to me. My book was more or less complete a long time back. But eversince things got finalised with Piyush, for the last 100 days or so I have been doing, redoing and doing each and every paragraph all over again. And at this point I feel like sharing a secret.

Being a management consultant myself, for these last 100 days I have been leading a double life. While on one hand I have been working my ever best on the book, getting it reviewed and reworking on it ; on the other hand I have been constantly working on its marketing efforts alongwith the rest of my team. The pre-launch advertisements and teasers with the challenging name CYCBTH have already started coming out. I want everything around this book to be as unique as possible. It should set new standards and guidelines for the Indian publishing industry. What excites me is that it seems our efforts have started paying results even before the launch... today itself I saw an Airtel ad. with a caption "Don't count your chickens before they hatch... not until your mobile tells you to." For me this is not just a book. I also look at it as a product, a future brand. That's why I said its a secret... I don't really feel like, how I guess, a typical author feels.

From the name of the book to the cover design to the balancing of examples with theories everything has been done with the help of endless sessions of brain storming and feedback. Everytime I read the book... I compared it with the Hindi blockbuster "Sholay". At the back of my mind, I want this book to be like "Sholay". That's my benchmark and that's what I want my book to be (a benchmark) for future authors writing books for the masses. On the subjects covered in the book I could perhaps talk atleast 25 times more but as a marketing man I realise the consumer is the king. I think very few people have understood the Indian consumer better than Ramesh Sippy did (during the making of Sholay), apart from a handful more like Yash Chopra and Alyque Padamsee etc. Thus, I have been telling my friends that while this book should have a simply written yet strong message portrayed through the characters of Sanjeev Kumar, Amitabh etc... it also needs to clearly define the main villain and bring his demonic behaviour (remember the typical "Kitne Aadmi

The?") in front of the readers and at the same time maintain the right mix of humour of Asrani, romance of Dharmendra - Hema and the short and thus acceptable dash of shimmer that Helen brought in. I hope I have been able to do justice to my thoughts.

Its a difficult task to strike such a perfect balance. But the reward is surely worth the effort. Madhavan, my editor has been a great support. The editing work, though, started first when I sent a few chapters of the book to Amit Agarwal, who pointed out many aspects which I had over looked. A. Sandeep took over and worked a lot on it. He has promised to help me make great changes for the international edition, since many things I have taken for granted for the Indian audience would need to be explained better for the international audience. I hope he keeps up his promise.

The final, the most detailed and most thoughtful part of the editing was done by none other than my first wife (the current and the only) Rajita. Between us, we don't thank each other too much. I love her. I am indebted to my father for giving me a complex-free upbringing which has helped me stay back in India and love it genuinely. Arundhati, my sister threatened me that I better thank her, so I better. She is too sweet and appreciating. Before ending I would like to apologise to my nine month old son, Che, for spending less time with him in the last few months while writing this book. I hope you grow up and find it an interesting read.

Arindam Chaudhuri
16.07.2001

Contents

If you Think
You Can,
You Are
Right

ALMOST ANYTHING YOU DO

WILL SEEM INSIGNIFICANT

BUT IT IS VERY IMPORTANT

THAT YOU DO IT...

YOU MUST BE THE CHANGE

YOU WISH TO SEE IN

THE WORLD.

If you think you can,
you are right
Just be passionate about what you think

They say "don't count your chickens before they
hatch". They are correct. Every time you are
about to sign a big contract in life, expect to meet with
a fatal accident while getting out of the car on your way
to signing the contract. In fact, every time you are
about to start the greatest speech or concert of your
life, expect to fall flat on the stage and break your nose
with blood spilled all over. Or rather, when your aircraft

has landed safely, don't start thanking God, but expect to die due to a fall from the stairs while climbing down the aircraft.

So what if you have written your exams to your utter satisfaction; don't rejoice, but anticipate that your paper will get exchanged with that of the worst student of your class. Have you worked very hard on the most important project of your life? Stay put. On the day of submission, your computer will be attacked by the latest virus which will eat up your whole project without a burp.

Believe me this is how every Tom, Dick and our very own Hari think. That is why they are called Tom, Dick and Hari and not **Gandhi, Lincoln and Gates**.

Life has its extremes and there are so many things which are beyond our control. Life itself, accidents, government policies... **and taxes of course**. But do you live expecting extremes to take control of your life? And then, expect success to be with you too?

I don't.

Most successful men and women don't.

Success is a matter of attitude. It is a matter of what you think you are capable of. It is a matter of futuristic thinking and planning. It is about doing things carefully. Instead of getting out of your car

without looking at the speeding car zooming towards you, you can be more careful. You can also climb down a little carefully so that you don't fall off the aircraft stairs. In fact, it is also about taking a couple of backups on your computer in case it is the most important project of your life.

And then it is about counting your chickens before they hatch... and about a positive attitude... and about believing that: "if you think you can, you are right".

Luckily, I have had the opportunity to interact with a lot of people who have been successful. Every meeting has been a learning experience for me. Apart from these interactions, I have also been extremely lucky to have had a grandmother who inculcated in me the habit of reading books from as far back as I can remember. Since the age of four, every night before going to sleep she used to read to me a Russian book for children. Soon a time came when I knew the book by heart and, inspite of not knowing how to read, I would take the book and keep reading it loudly, turning the pages at the right points as if I could read. Of course, later in life my father saw to it that I further developed this habit. He is one of the most innovative men I know. He declared an incentive of 15 paise for each page that I would read when I was in the sixth standard.

This incentive system continued till I cleared my tenth board exams, and it was only when he realised that reading had become my passion that he started giving me pocket money which was not linked to my reading habit. Why I mention this incident is because it is impossible to experience everything by oneself and reading fills up this gap.

Today, I realise that I know a lot of MBAs, Ph.Ds and engineers, yet very few are half as educated as my grandmother. Many of these brilliantly educated people begin to stammer on the mention of authors like Victor Hugo, etc., people whom my grandmother keeps quoting every now and then! At the age of 85, she still reads books regularly from our locality library. Whenever I have felt helpless about not being able to interact with a great personality in person (dead or alive), I have somehow managed to fill the vacuum by reading about the person.

With all that I have gained by way of my reading and interaction, as I sit back trying to jot down the most important factors that contributed to these success stories, many parameters emerged convincing me that you can

> **But do we live expecting extremes to take control of our life? And then, expect success to be with us too?**

count your chickens before they hatch. I realised that it's all about **attitude, learning from mistakes, persisting in the face of adversity, vision, empathy for others, human relation skills, communication skills...**

This book will talk about all this and more.

I think that there are three dimensions to success. One of our professors at *Indian Institute of Planning and Management* (IIPM), Sumit Chaudhuri loves calling it the **ASK principle of success**. The **Attitude** dimension, the **Skill** dimension and the **Knowledge** dimension. **Almost always in that order.** You might have (and many people do have) all the knowledge in the world and yet fail to achieve anything due to the lack of skills, most often in dealing with others, and the right attitude. There are the second set of people who have the knowledge as well as the skill but **altitudes elude them due to the lack of an attitude.** The combination of these three makes a Mahatma: The Gandhi.

Why I said 'almost always in that order' is because the reverse is not true. For, I have seen plenty of success stories where people without high degrees of knowledge and skill achieve great heights due to their attitude. So, that makes attitude the most important dimension.

This book will deal with success in three parts— **Attitude,** which is covered in this chapter, **Skill,** on which the next two chapters will concentrate, and lastly **Knowledge**, to which I have devoted the last two chapters. The last two chapters would also focus on aspects of "Theory 'i' Management" which provides knowledge and insight about India centric management ideas for achieving success and helping you count your chickens before they hatch...

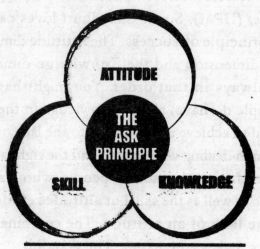

The 3 dimensions to success

Now to dwell more on attitudes...

Friends of Sabeer Bhatia (the former owner of hotmail.com) say, when he had nothing they used to be amused at his ability to think big. No doubt he made it big more by his attitude than anything else. Inspite of poor financial background with many adversities,

Abraham Lincoln's attitude was always rich and right. The urge to make it big made **Vidyasagar** study under a lamp-post, and he reached the echelons of learning inspite of all odds.

In his first year in the automobile business, this man went bankrupt and two years later his second company also failed... but he did not give up. His third, however, has made him a household name. It's the right attitude that helped **Henry Ford** achieve global success.

A professor of mine had an extraordinary success ratio with training students for IAS studies. He used to say that apart from academics he used to focus extensively on creating a positive mental attitude in the student. Thus, from the day anybody came to him he had to repeat the words "I can make it, I shall make it and I will make it" at least 25 times a day. He says, students later on said that this focus on "right attitude development" is what actually made the difference between them and the others who could not make it to the IAS.

While on one hand the constant positive attitude in the Kennedy family was the key behind **John F. Kennedy's** success story; on the other hand, the constant negative reinforcements and negative family influences from his early childhood is what made **Oswald** grow up to become what he became: the murderer of Kennedy.

In fact, upon looking at these examples closely, one will realise that attitude has one key dimension. A dimension that is rarely talked about. A dimension I thought of when I saw the **complete lack of enthusiasm** in the employees of many of the Indian and multinational organisations I have been interacting with during my training programmes—and that dimension is **passion**.

There are people with skills, and with knowledge and with an urge to succeed but somehow the urge is not forceful enough. RATHER, NOT PASSIONATE ENOUGH.

Add to this the fact that the employees are not committed to their organisations (no wonder my firm's recruitment outfit is so successful!) makes it seem so ironical that these very organisations expect to succeed with such manpower.

Thus, I say, right attitude is all about being passionate about what you do. Passion works wonders. From Henry Ford to J.F.Kennedy, everyone mentioned here saw success because they were passionate about their work.

Did you know about the man who passionately believed that he could make a difference to the sufferings of people around. Stories of the Ramayan and the Mahabharat narrated by his mother left an indelible impression on his mind. He developed traits such as courage, sympathy for the poor and an urge to do something great. In 1888, **Narendranath** finally left his home and travelled as an unknown mendicant. With a burning desire to know India better and to do something for the oppressed, he went from place to place.

[
You know
what you are,
but not
What you can
become
]

He said, **"the greatest sin is to think of yourself as weak"**. He decided to go to the West to seek help for the poor of India and thus gave shape to his life's mission. His journey to America commenced on 31st May 1893. He came back to India on 20th February 1897, **TRIUMPHANT**. He was no more the unknown Sanyasi. He was now **Swami Vivekananda**—one of India's all-time great spiritual leaders whose teachings, even today, inspire millions. What happened in Chicago is known to all. Swami Vivekananda had the courage, conviction and most importantly the passion to follow his dreams and fulfill them; the passion to count his chickens before they hatched.

Remember **To achieve greatness you also have to be passionate about your beliefs.**

It is like the story of the young boy who in 1938, while at school, had begun to develop his unique concept of a piston. He tried hard to sell his work to *Toyota Corporation* but was rejected again and again. He was sent back to school and his friends laughed at his crazy attempts. Two years later he got the contract. His passion and belief in what he was doing paid off since he knew what he wanted and worked hard on it till he got the exact number of chickens he had planned for. When the Japanese government refused to give him concrete to build a factory due to wartime shortages, he along with his team invented a process to make their own concrete. At the end of the war when a gasoline crisis hit Japan, **Mr. Honda** attached a small motor to his cycle and later decided to build a plant that would build motors for his new invention, the motorcycle.

If you think you can, you are right. But think passionately. All stories of success have one common element: passion. **Passion** for what they want to achieve. **Enough passion** to keep their eyes from wandering away from the goal. **Total passion** to finally see them through.

Passionate beliefs often make great sacrifices look easy and are the foundation of success. Named Siddhartha by his family, he grew up to believe that happiness was not inside the four walls of the palace where he resided. At the age of 29, to follow his urge for knowledge, soon after the birth of his son Rahula, he left his wife, son and kingdom to be one with the sufferings of normal human beings. After going through hardship and pain he finally experienced enlightenment. More than 1500 years after his enlightenment, the Talibans may be out to destroy his statues, but Buddhism remains one of the strongest religions in the world. The statues that are engraved in the souls of his followers cannot be destroyed. **Gautam Buddha** had the courage to revolt against the ills of Hinduism, namely the caste system, etc., and the conviction to go in search of something new, the chickens that no one knew existed!

Those who can count their chickens before they hatch are people who are passionate about seeing the maximum number of chickens hatching!

Success comes to people who are passionate about it and passion has its own principles and guidelines.

You might be right at the top but are you one of those who constantly need to be motivated by others or do you fall into the category of people who are self-driven and passionate about their work? If you belong to the former category and have by default made it to the top, mark my words you could be a menace to your organisation. Any CEO/President, and for that matter anybody with an urge to succeed, should invariably fall into the latter category. Sadly my experience with the corporate world shows the reverse. Demotivated, overstressed, unable to strike a balance between work and family, looking for a change, feeling helpless about the environment and feeling that the compensation package is not good enough are some of the most common characteristics of today's managers and specially those at the very top.

What you have therefore is an organisation which is being led by people who are not driven enough and as a result we are where we are...

> # You see things
> # and say: WHY?
> # But I dream of things
> # that never were,
> # and say: WHY NOT?
> ## — *Bernard Shaw*

I feel that this problem is essentially due to the fact that modern day people seem to be passionless. **We don't work with passion, we don't play with passion, we don't eat with passion, we don't listen to music with passion, our paintings lack passion, we don't express passionately, and, as a recent study points out, our** lovemaking has also lost passion. This material world of passionless people is destroying our zeal for life.

We have stopped celebrating life. The solution lies in looking at things around us more intensely, feeling them more passionately and cultivating within us an urge to celebrate life. If you don't have a/any passion, develop it. One day while I was talking to the CEO of *Electrolux*, India, Mr. Ram S Ramasundar, he explained that he did not believe that there was any work which could not be made interesting and involving... one just needed to put his heart into it. The Managing Director of *Hughes Escorts*, Mr. Arun Kumar, too came up with the same conclusion and he finds the lack of passion a big problem in the Indian corporate sector.

Therefore I always advise my clients to take people based upon their **PQ (Passion Quotient)**, that we at *Planman* have developed, instead of their IQ. There is a big difference between people who just work and people who work passionately. And this difference is the difference between success and failure.

People who are passionate about their work are a boon to organisations, as they are high achievers and always remain self-driven and motivated. They are so involved in their work that once they have determined their goals they are prepared to try different approaches. They are more goal-oriented than technique-oriented.

For them, the method of choice is the method which will work best, not necessarily the usual method. If the common sense approach does not work, they will invent a new one. They are creative people, not necessarily in the sense of being artists or musicians but in the sense of being ingenious, adaptable and innovative with whatever is at hand to solve the problem to achieve the objective.

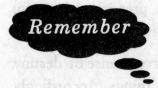 **People with passion automatically tend to be innovative.**

In the early 50's, officials in the treasury of the Arabian Kingdom of Yemen found the main unit of their currency, solid silver coins called the Rial, disappearing from circulation. They were all going to Aden, where a mere clerk in a British Trading Company had put an open order for all of them. He had realised that selling them after melting them down was more valuable than the value of Rial. He made some money before it was officially stopped. This money added to the money he had already saved helped him start off as a trader in polyester yarn. Today, **Dhirubhai Ambani...** is the most powerful business tycoon in India. All this in one generation. Because he has been innovative as well as passionate about his dreams.

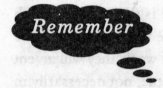

People with passion look forward towards unique accomplishments and are oriented towards the future.

Successful people may not necessarily have a clear idea of their long-term goals, they address themselves with maximum effort to the task of the moment, with an underlying feeling that in some way successful accomplishment of their task is preparing them for more important activities in the future.

Perhaps it can be said that they have a sense of destiny, i.e. they are destined for bigger things. Accordingly, each current task, no matter how minor, is perceived as important in itself because of its relationship to their growth process and preparation for the future. This feeling of destiny gives rise to a feeling of self-confidence and the willingness to make decisions and take responsibility.

It was this urge for being unique that made a young boy stand at the centre of the Sydney cricket ground and tell his father "I shall never be satisfied until I play on this ground" and then not just playing there but creating history. He was passionate about his game and ended his career with a record average of 99.96 runs. The Don is what people lovingly used to call Sir Don Bradman.

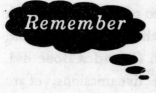

Remember

The highest levels of passionate efforts have been outcomes of great ideologies and visions. These efforts on their own have the ability to become legendary regardless of their results.

Ché Guevara, the world's greatest ever revolutionary (who was described by none other than the great Frenchman **Satre** as not only an intellectual but also the most complete human being of our age), always felt **"that your failure does not necessarily mean that the cause you were fighting for was not worth it"**. Inspite of being an Argentine, he went to Cuba and fought its battle of independence for the sake of his ideology. And then quit his top ministerial posts in Cuba to fight for African countries before coming back to Bolivia and meeting his end. Ché failed in most of his wars against oppressors, yet he achieved what he always wanted.

A graffiti scrawl in Spanish on the wall of the public telephone office in the little town of Vallegrande in Bolivia where he was executed reads: **"Ché – Alive as they never wanted you to be"**. He remains today in the heart of millions of people across the world as a revolutionary icon... a folk hero of mythical proportions. He dared to have an Utopian dream...and chase it. That's what counting your chickens before they hatch is all about. Che dared to dream the dream of bringing independence with the help of a new and brave army just the way **Subash Chandra Bose** did. Both of them failed in their respective missions, yet are counted amongst the world's greatest leaders. They were successful in moving the thought processes of an entire generation with the ideology and vision they were passionately committed to.

So, you might count your chickens before they hatch and finally see that your calculations were wrong. Yet, if you had chased what you believed in, a few chickens less here and there would not actually matter in the final count, for success is not just about achieving what you wanted but more about making an attempt to achieve what you believed in.

It is about **being a woman and leading a battle** of heroic proportions in the South-East Asian nation of Burma, where on one hand is the state law-and-order restoration council, and on the other a diminutive 51-year old mother of two, named **Aung San Suu Kyi**. She is leading her people in a non-violent struggle for democracy a struggle which has also won her a Nobel peace prize.

It is about **walking thousands of kilometers for the sake of your ideals and people**. The Chinese revolution (popularly known as **The Long March**) under the fiercely committed leadership of **Mao Tse Tung** achieved exactly that... and about the foresight and vision to lead the largest country in the world (Russia) out of the clutches of the tyrannical Tzars through **single-minded determination** the way **Vladimir Ilyich Lenin** did.

And, then, it is about dreaming of taking a country on the path to freedom after years of exploitation. It is about putting your life at stake for this cause and ending up becoming a Mahatma: **Mahatma Gandhi**.

Remember

People who passionately believe "they can" develop the ability to persist in the face of adversity.

They are not easily discouraged by failure. The underlying self-confidence helps them to carry on despite setbacks. They use failure as a learning experience. They never leave a task unfinished. They feel tense as long as there is something undone. But when it becomes clear that the odds against them have become too high they have no hesitation in quitting and shifting tactics.

These people **are never completely content**. They are not satisfied with the status quo nor are they satisfied with what they have achieved. Their standards are high and as soon as they attain one goal they set their sights on a new goal, perhaps a little more difficult one. They also want to know the result of their efforts. They want some objective measure of what they are doing, which should be available soon after the action is taken. Not only is this feedback stimulating and satisfactory, it also helps them to adjust and improve their efforts.

They are also said to **live "in-process"**. They do not require a complete structuring of a situation in order to function. They are better able to tolerate ambiguity. They always have some project underway with so much enthusiasm that they feel the lack of time to get it all done. Their enmity with time is very open. They look at time as a binding chain or an obstacle.

Successful people don't like being bound by routines and schedules. They exemplify this tendency by describing time as "a galloping horse", "a bird in flight", "a fleeing thief". They are active, restless. They are not content to sit quietly. They like to take the initiative. They are pioneers, adventurers, willing to leave the present and venture into the unknown. It shows not only in terms of ideas but also in terms of physical action. Someone said that the epitaph of these type of people could be:

> **"Here I lie in my final condition**
> **Let it be said, I tested tradition"**

They are always on the hunt for the chickens that never hatched...

When the dream of becoming a famous musician almost seemed lost, the only thing that drove Billy Joel ahead in life was his girlfriend. When she too deserted him, he was almost about to commit suicide when better sense prevailed and he got himself admitted into a mental hospital. He came out and went on to become what he is known for and later recalled saying "Oh I will never get that low again".

Remember

Great passions can defy destiny.

When you chase your dreams, there can be only two outcomes. Either you make it or you give up. And when the chickens you expect to hatch don't hatch and you end up being paralysed from the neck below since the age of 14, the easier option is to give up and focus on your pain. **Ed Roberts** refused to do that. Instead he mastered how to lead a normal life battling passionately against all odds.

From his wheelchair he became the first disabled Director of California State Department of Rehabilitation. He chased the chickens which did not hatch and got them… because he did not give up and believed that **"impossible is not a word in my dictionary"** (as **Napoleon** said).

Like the great scientist who has been suffering from the early 1960s from a progressive and incurable motor-neuron disease that now confines him to a wheel chair. Of this illness **Stephen Hawking** says that it has enhanced his career by giving him the freedom to think about physics and the universe. He has been proving correct what another legend **Albert Einstein** once said: **"what is essential in the existence of a man of my type is what he thinks and how he thinks, and not what he does or how he suffers"**.

"Counting your chickens before they hatch" is thus about believing passionately in the two words: **I CAN**.

It is about being blind since birth and yet having the conviction that you can make it and becoming a **Stevie Wonder**. It is about being deaf and composing some of the best and profoundest music ever, like **Beethoven** did. It is about not only being blind and deaf but also being dumb and becoming a **Helen Keller**.

It is about being kicked out of school and then becoming the world's leading business tycoon and changing the way the world works, like **Bill Gates** has done.

In fact, it is about **failing** in business at the age of 21, being **defeated** in a legislative election at the age of 22, overcoming the **death** of his sweetheart at the age of 26, **losing** congressional races at the ages of 34 and 36, losing the senatorial race at the age of 45 and, again later at the age of 49, **losing** the race for the vice-presidential post at the age of 47, **and finally becoming the President of United States at the age of 52! It is about being Abraham Lincoln.** All these events—which to a common man would seem to be failures—were to Abraham Lincoln stepping stones to a future that he passionately dreamt of.

Remember **People with passion for work generally have the courage to whistle while they work.**

These people enjoy their work thoroughly. They laugh while at work without any guilt for they know that they give 100% to their work. Thus, they like to take personal responsibility. When they undertake a task they prefer to have it clearly understood that they will see it through. **They want to take credit for the success, but are equally prepared to accept the blame for failure.** They are not "buck-passers". They do not blame their subordinates or the government.

They like games of skill over games of chance because they feel no control over the outcome of the latter.

YOU CAN FAIL
your way to success

EVEN NAPOLEON LOST

one third of all the important

battles he fought

They are people who might fail..., fail **9999 times** and yet with a smile say **"I learnt 9999 times how not to make an electric bulb..."**. And after many more such attempts **Thomas Edison** did invent the electric bulb and went on to create, way back in 1879, an organisation (*General Electric*) which even today stands tall. In fact, he ended up earning more than 1000 patents for inventions including the phonograph, the incandescent electric lamp, the motion picture projector, etc.

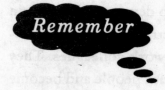

People with passion for work have all their senses involved in the job at hand.

These people work not just with their brains—their eyes work, their ears work and their overall expressions work. You look at them and you know that passion is at work. They often give their work more preference over bodily needs. That doesn't mean that they ignore bodily needs but while at work they often forget when it is time for lunch etc. Work often is their lunch.

They know even at a tender age of 12 what they want to do for the rest of their lives like this young Yugoslavian girl knew. She worked passionately towards her goal. Her bodily needs took second priority over the hunger and abject poverty she saw in people around. She became the most admired woman of all time and served the poorest of poor tirelessly throughout her life. She went on to become a mother to all. Yes, for **Mother Teresa** work was often her lunch.

These people with passion for work usually demonstrate some interpersonal competence and enjoy long-term relationships.

They recognise the importance of interpersonal relationships in achieving most objectives; therefore they devote reasonable efforts to develop and maintain adequate relationships with others. They are often task-oriented and select experts as work colleagues. They are highly capable of working with people and become a **J.R.D. Tata**—one of the few people known for his ability of having great faith in the capabilities of others and make them achieve success.

One does need to remember that passion for work can be maintained only by developing a habit of taking reasonable challenges.

This is a key behavioural trait of people who achieve success. They neither like excessive odds against their success nor too easy tasks. The reasonable possibility of failure excites them to put in increased efforts. **They want to stretch to put in that extra bit to achieve their goal**.

On the other hand, people lacking passion prefer an easy task to ensure success and avoid chances of failure. Otherwise they take very high-risk tasks so that they can make it clear to the world that the task was so difficult and the odds against it so high that no one could really have achieved it. Their fear of failure thus is very high. People with passion at work enjoy calculated risks when they feel they are up against a worthy adversary. The element of reasonable challenge helps them maintain their passion levels at work.

[Be not afraid of growing slowly, be afraid only of standing still]

Charles Dickens went through abject poverty and adversity in life. People kept rejecting his work. However, he was sure about what he was aiming for and, since he believed in himself and he knew that he had a fair chance of making it, he could sustain his passion for writing. Success could not elude him for long, and the 15 major stories and countless short stories he wrote and the characters and places he wrote about will live with us for ever. Probably Charles Dickens is a classic example of a person who could count his chickens before they hatched. A person who passionately believed in the two words—**I CAN**.

"We can characterise people with a passionate attitude for work as restless, energetic, striving for, seeking and enjoying challenges. For them, life is a reasonable adventure"

People with the above characteristics tend to be passionate, self-driven and motivated, have a positive attitude towards life and are high achievers. They can maintain their passions and levels of motivation through their own enthusiasm, restlessness and zeal to achieve more. They end up achieving what they set out for since their targets don't have high risk, but nor are these targets with no risk so as to make life dull. Their targets always have moderate risks to keep the challenge in life alive and thus they are able to keep their passion levels high and don't need to be motivated by others. They are invaluable assets for any organisation.

SOME EMPIRICAL EVIDENCE

In the early 60s Srully Blotnick did a research on 1500 people. These people were divided into two groups and observed for 20 years. Group A made up 83% of the sample and Group B the rest 17%. While the former lot embarked on a career chosen for the reason of making money, the latter chose a career based upon their passions and did what they wanted to do. In 1982, he published his research in Playboy Paperbacks *Getting Rich Your Own Way*. At the end of 20 years, 101 people had become millionaires. Out of them, 100 were from the group which decided to follow their passions.

Passion at work can also reduce the risk of getting a heart disease. A study done by Massachusetts HEW investigating the cause of heart diseases, asked the participants two questions: Are you happy? Do you love your work? Results showed that those who answered Yes to both the questions had a better chance of not getting a heart disease.

In IIPM, we have a course called "Art of Living" where we invite successful people to talk about their experiences with life. From Satish Gujral to Shobhna Narayan, from Vasant Sathe to Birju Maharaj and from Gita Chandran to Anil Maetri, whoever has come, has left with me an everlasting feeling that **success, happiness, and very often even money is directly related to just one thing—passion at work.**

INCULCATING PASSION

I realise that with more and more IT orientation, mechanisation and division of labour has alienated man from his work. He is a small part of the final product and fails to identify himself with the final output. This is sad and therefore I have been also talking about my concept of **"Happy Capitalism"**. I developed this concept of Happy Capitalism, looking at the growing need for humanising the capitalistic economy in which we live.

While on one hand I appreciate many aspects of capitalism and realise it is an inevitable force; I also feel that while chasing too much in a free-market economy, we often tend to ignore more important issues conducive to human happiness (other than material satisfaction).

Thus, happy capitalism amongst other things is about small-scale entrepreneurship, social sector entrepreneurship **(any social commitment invariably increases passion at work)**. It is about building small organisations with high involvement levels. If you are getting paid Rs. 20,000 at your job, maybe it is because you are giving your company Rs. 2 lakhs of returns. Most likely with such abilities you could become an entrepreneur **(countries like India are desperately** seeking your hidden entrepreneurial talent), earn more, identify better with your work and display passion and enthusiasm at work (in case right now you don't seem to find passion at work).

Of course this is a very simple summarisation of the concept of Happy Capitalism. It incorporates many other aspects relating to life, work and economics (I would be soon writing a book on the same incorporating the details about this concept of Happy Capitalism).

For others who for various reasons are unable to become entrepreneurs, there are other ways of achieving similar levels of passion and commitment. After Hiroshima and Nagasaki, the Japanese become passionate—even one who was fixing screws on the door of a Toyota car, not because his job was exciting but because he was passionately patriotic and he wanted to see his cars take over the American roads one day. **Patriotism enhances passion at work.**

At _Honda_, workers are proud to call themselves "Honda Men". **Identification with the vision of the organisation increases passion at work.**

Martin Luther King Jr. said that if you are a street sweeper, so be it—but clean your street so well that others are forced to acknowledge your existence and feel that "here lived a street sweeper who did his job well". We need to realise that often the job we do is out of our own choice, so it is best to do it well. **"Thus, anything worth doing is worth doing passionately."**

If you fail to achieve passion at work due to circumstances, beyond your control, nobody can stop you from **developing a passion after work. This can often help you work with more enthusiasm,** for one can overcome the boredom of a routine by looking forward to other passions. There are doctors whose passion at work increases because they play the piano after work; there are CEOs whose passion at work increases because they play golf after work; and there are managers who start enjoying work after a vacation at a resort (in this case appreciating nature is the underlying passion).

During an interaction with the Managing Director of *Thomas Cook*, Mr. Ashwani Kakkar, I was taken aback by the number of things he was passionate about. He has a personal collection of paintings and art objects which would do a national museum proud. He mixes his own music. Ask him and he is quick to reply that these passions help him work more creatively.

A man comes back home totally tired and is in no mood to do anything, yet when his friend calls him out for a game of football he plays for the next two hours as if he was totally fresh and energetic. Ever wondered why?

I want to conclude by asking you to not to be under any misconception that the people I have talked about in this chapter never knew where they wanted to be. Not only did they know what they wanted but they are people who believed passionately that "they can". They dared to count their chickens before they hatch and script their own success stories.

Can you?

End note: If you think you can, you are right. Just be passionate about it. And if you lack passion, then develop it because success never comes till you are passionate about it.

Friends whom you will meet in hell

Friends whom you will meet in hell

The prerequisites for motivating people & winning friends

H ell is where most of us reach at the end of this journey and that's where best friends seem to unite again! But let me tell you it's not easy to make such lasting impressions so as to carry your friendship to hell! It requires a lot of talent and carefully-practised human relation skills. Sadly for

me and fortunately for the entire mankind a man by
the name of **Dale Carnegie** wrote a book called *How
to Win Friends and Influence People*. Sadly for me because
all I can ever think of writing on motivating others
or winning friends has been written by him in this
book. Fortunately for the entire mankind because
never before or never after has a better book been
written on human relations. This chapter is for those
who haven't read his book and also for those who
have, since it's always good to read great ideas more
than once.

This and the next chapter have been devoted by me
to the key skills that I find most necessary for people
to succeed in life. No prizes for guessing that these
are essentially human relation skills. The first skill
that I will concentrate upon in this chapter is about
the art of winning friends and motivating others.
The second skill that I would focus upon in the next
chapter is about developing good communication
skills. Rarely would you find success stories associated
with individuals who do not possess these skills.

Personally speaking, I don't like to hear motivation
speeches from people who don't give a damn about
their own people. You will be surprised to find out
the high manpower turnover ratios in the
organisations run by some of the most popular

motivational speakers. The first lesson is that knowing is not good enough. Practising it wholeheartedly is what matters, because going by the number of copies sold of Dale Carnegie's masterpiece, and assuming that each reader practised it on ten others and motivated them to practise it further—the world would have been a great place to live in!

I don't have many áchievements to boast of. But when it comes to "people skills", I can proudly say that three of my friends from the age of five still remain very close to me. At the age of nine we shifted to a new house with a park in front of it. All I did since then was cultivate friendships. Five of my best friends, I made then... way back in 1980, are still as close to me and are the pillars of my organisation. Ashok Bose, due to unfortunate circumstances, never got to complete his studies. Today, he manages all the establishment aspects of my organisation with such finesse and command that no one would ever believe his past. Sandeep Ghosh, who at one point of time could have matured into a known vagabond, today is the administrative head of my firm and the most respected and loved person. Sujit Roy (or Bunty, as we lovingly call him) was into everything that one can't write about. Today, he is the head of the CEO Search Division of our consulting firm with its headquarters in Delhi. Now, he has a reputation of

People Power Philosophy

LET'S LOVE PEOPLE

and use material things
Instead of loving material things and using people

it's the people power which decides your future

ARINDAM CHAUDHURI

constantly over-achieving his targets. Bireshwar Dey, who no one thought would ever make it, today is the finance head of all my activities. Prashanto Banerji, who was the pace bowler of our cricket team, is today married to my sister Arundhati and teaches appreciation of literature, art and culture as a part of our MBA course in IIPM.

Sujit, Bireshwar and Prashanto did pursue their MBA too from our institute. When I joined the institute in the year 1989, I met Sandeep. After doing our course and working with us for a year, he went on to do his MBA from IIM, Calcutta. Everybody said he would never come back. After completing his studies at IIM he did not even sit for a single campus interview. He was back and today is the consulting partner in my firm. Prasoon Majumdar was different. After doing his MBA with me, he was always in touch with me, but, like most MBAs, was bitten by the corporate bug. Nevertheless in 1999, he joined us. Today, as the head of our Economics department, he is one of the most loved professors at IIPM.

One after another of my students, now my friends, left the option of opting for a corporate career in order to join me on the basis of a future made up of only words (when I started *Planman* with no credentials to boast off, the only thing I could promise them were distant dreams). **Most of them have never thought of leaving and are contributing to my firm's ambitious growth targets.** My firm is today made up of seven of my past friends and about a hundred and ten of my students.

I think I know a few things about winning friends and keeping them. The things I knew I later read in Dale Carnegie's book too. But I maintain I knew them before I read the book. I knew them because I sincerely wanted to maintain my friends and honestly loved them. I knew them because **everybody who is honest and sincere about others knows them. It comes naturally.** Yet, I will discuss them more.

At home, when we were growing up, **I remember distinctly the excessive amount of importance my dad used to lay on SMILING.** He used to take feedback from all of us on who used to smile the most. At a later age, the competition had become useless, since my brother Aurobindo had become the established winner. What I am trying to say is that nothing can be more pleasing than a good smile. It's a great way to make a terrific first impression. A smile can say 'I really like you' and 'you make me happy' or 'it's great to see you'... Actions can often speak louder than words.

My son, Ché (I named him after Ché Guevara. In fact his full name is Ché Kabir Chaudhuri and I hope one day he will bring about revolutionary changes that Ché dreamt of, through peaceful, secular and coexistential means that **Kabir** used to believe in) has been smiling whenever he sees me from the age of one and a half months. He can't speak yet (he is nine months old now) but he has been telling me everything I want to hear with his smiles. **Smiles speak.** I come home tired and his smile brings all my energy back. Something that my dad also talks about... even today with a big smile. In 1972, he was posted in Mumbai. We used to stay in a hotel since the company had not been able to arrange any accommodation till then. It seems everyday when my dad would come back from the office, I would be standing on the stairs with a big smile and jumping around. It is something that all the other guests in the hotel as well as my dad used to enjoy very much. No wonder, he still talks about it so fondly.

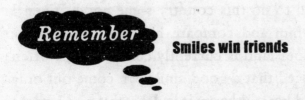

Remember   **Smiles win friends**

Research shows people who smile have the ability to win friends, manage, teach and sell more effectively.

They also raise happier children! Unfortunately, a recent research which I happened to read, done by a Swedish foundation on laughter, shows that people in the developed world used to laugh and smile much more forty years ago but now they just "chuckle", and that too for only six minutes a day. For one of our regular official excursion trips, I had taken some of my other friends who don't work with us. Back from the trip, these friends had just one thing to conclude about my organisation. We laugh too much. And they wish it would come to them as naturally too. I say, "smile!", it helps.

Talking about smiles, it would be unfair to not mention about one of the most charismatic of leaders India has ever produced. His smile accentuated his charisma. He had the ability to stand next to any world leader and outshine them with his smile. Although, perhaps, he understood less about economics and the running of our country, **Rajiv Gandhi** with his smile at least made us feel that he had the will to do this country some good. When I remember him and compare him with most other politicians our land is currently cursed with, I often feel convinced that a good smile can come out only from a good heart. I know it is debatable and I might be wrong, but, scams or no scams, my instincts tell me that people like Rajiv Gandhi and **Kapil Dev**...

with their wholehearted smiles, must be great at heart. That's the power of a smile. On a personal note, I may add that the thing which perhaps attracts me most towards people (women included!) is their smiles and you bet my wife has a genuine smile; good enough to keep us going strong, with each passing day!

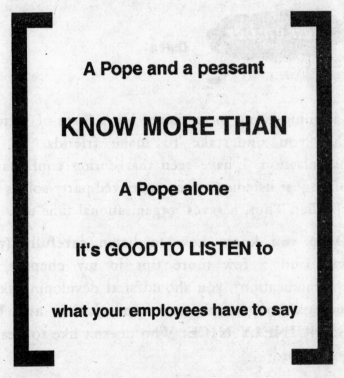

A Pope and a peasant

KNOW MORE THAN

A Pope alone

It's GOOD TO LISTEN to

what your employees have to say

The next thing I have realised as a very important factor in winning friends is about the great quality of 'listening', something that most of us tend to ignore so often.

It is the best way to have a conversation. **If you want to make friends—LISTEN**. Listen intently, listen genuinely and if you do so the other person is surely going to love you. As the saying goes **"few human beings are proof against the implied flattery of rapt attention"**.

Listen

Listening is not mere silence but a form of activity that you undertake to make friends. In my organisation, I have seen that during conflicts so often just listening to the aggrieved party solves the conflict. Thus, it saves organisational time too.

Once you know how to listen carefully (you will find a few more tips in my chapter on communication), you should start developing skills on how to give **sincere appreciation and BE GENUINELY NICE:** Who doesn't like to hear a good word?

If you want friends, learn to shower honest praise on them.

People love being appreciated provided it is sincere. There are people who just can't say something good to others, and then they wonder why they have no friends!

Moving another step forward, it is also important **NOT TO MAKE THE OTHER PERSON FEEL LIKE A LOSER**. It is the best way to avoid uneasiness between friends. It's really important that you never say "you are wrong" to others.

It is said that if you can be sure of being right 55% of the time, you can go to Wall Street and make a million dollars a day. If you can't be sure of being right even 55% of the time, why should you tell other people that they are wrong.

Remember

Call attention to other people's mistakes indirectly after showing respect to the other persons' opinions.

Knowing all the above is not enough. My dad, who spent most of his youth in Europe doing all his higher studies, always says that the difference between a European and an Indian is that a European says thank you and sorry much more easily. It seems we Indians are not thankful about anything or sorry about anything either!

But, if you want friends, then whenever you are at fault, admit it quickly.

The best way is to rectify your mistakes quickly and retain friends. It is said that any fool can try to defend his or her mistakes—and most fools do. But, if you can admit your mistakes you give yourself a feeling of nobility and exultation. We should always remember that by fighting we can never get enough friends, but by yielding we get more than we can expect.

While dealing with people I never forget one very important principle—of trying to put myself in the other person's shoes

> **If you can admit your mistakes you can give yourself a feeling of nobility and exultation**

and understanding his part of the bargain. There are times when you feel that the other person has committed the biggest mistake of his life and he should not be spared. But, before blasting him, do try to find out his point of view.

I remember reading in Tagore's biography one incident which shook me completely. On one important day Tagore's old faithful servant did not turn up. When he came later in the evening, Tagore gave him a piece of his mind. The old faithful servant was very apologetic and told Tagore that he had come straight from the cremation ground after performing the last rites of his young son who had died that morning.

Do you see a paradigm shift happening inside you already? The same happened with me, when I read this tragic story. Today, as a matter of principle, I find out things from the other person's point of view before passing any judgement. **In a country like India, where we regularly deal with the poor and less fortunate people working for us, this becomes all the more important.**

 *Remember* **The rich have much. The poor have only feelings and self-respect.**

The ease with which we tend to assume that anything missing must have been stolen by the poor maid is shocking. When we do discover the missing thing later from some corner of our house, rarely do we go and apologise. We should follow the rule, let a thousand guilty get away unpunished but let not one innocent be punished (similar to what the Laws for punishing people keep talking about), especially so if the person is poor. Secondly, if we have made a mistake, we should apologise unconditionally. Apologising makes us greater individuals.

Most of us have a very short-sighted approach towards life. **The people we love most and people who love us most are the people to whom we are rude most often** just because we can take them for granted. I would often blast my brother for small nothings and never bother to apologise. Devoted that he was, he would blindly do everything I said, even if it meant going in the middle of the night and repairing the punctured tyre of my car (which I would leave somewhere in the middle of nowhere and come back home in a cab) and getting it back home.

Then one afternoon, I was watching a movie when suddenly and frantically my mother' called me downstairs. I ran down and she was screaming and crying that a phone call had come that my brother had died in an accident.

What was I left with? **Death is a great leveller.** Just when you think everything is under your control, it comes like a slap from someone up there to tell you, "Look! In this universe the earth itself is such a tiny identity, and within that invisible tiny identity you are a tinier microscopic identity—don't think too much of yourself". And suddenly you realise that the person you loved most is no more and you can't even apologise for the mistakes you committed. It can happen to anybody, any time.

Check out that you give maximum happiness to people you love most.

MOTIVATION is a slightly different cup of tea, though. It is not just about winning friends; it's also about driving people and friends towards higher levels of efforts on any job in hand (at home, in the club or at the office). Have you ever wondered how a two-year old kid on his birthday party has his eyes fixed on the birthday cake? And given the first opportunity jumps on the cake and smudges it all over his face. The same boy at the age of eight takes a big piece of cake and goes slyly to one corner of the house and eats it up. If by chance his sister comes asking for a bite, he spits on the piece of

> **It is not just about winning friends; it's also about driving people and friends towards higher levels of efforts**

cake and says that it has become dirty and she cannot have it ! At the age of fifteen, though, he carefully cuts out a big piece and goes towards his sister and gives it to her best friend standing next to her. Needless to mention that this friend is a girl. At another age, as the President of a large corporation, now a big man, he spends time ordering a big five-storeyed

PEOPLE are a company's
only sustainable competitive advantage
MOTIVATE THEM
You'll be surprised to see how fast
motivated people can run

cake which rolls on into the party in a big trolley. He cuts the cake but seems hardly interested in eating it or giving it to his secretary standing next to him (his wife obviously would not take it nicely). As an old man, he does not even remember his birthday. His children and his grandchildren remember, celebrate, cut a cake and give him the biggest piece. He, however, spots a little doll in the party and gives the piece to her, sees her spoil her clothes while trying to eat the cake, and he enjoys the scene.

The same cake. Different motives. Motivation is all about finding out the need inside a person, which, if satisfied, will make him exert high levels of efforts. **Once identified, all a good leader needs to do is satisfy it and see his people performing at high levels of productivity.**

For any organisation, whether a small one-room office in a remote town or a swanky multistoreyed giant at Backbay Reclamation, Mumbai, success and organisational performance is contingent on how well their respective employees perform. Scientists like **F. W. Taylor** have worked upon various aspects of how to scientifically attune people for better performance. We have witnessed the emergence and usage of some such scientific methods like job analysis, manpower planning, etc. for optimising human performance.

However critical such methods might be for regularising the human resources in an organisation, they do not necessarily guarantee better performance.

The reader might have by now noticed my repeated usage of the term 'performance'. It is because performance is a critical test of motivation. Performance of any individual is a function of his ability and willingness. The scientific methods of human resource management ensures that the right people get the right job. It is however motivation which sparks up the energies and activates the willingness of individuals.

Before I proceed to take up some critical issues of motivation, let me take the reader through a guided tour to understand the process of motivation. Referring back to my statements, let me start by saying that motivation is the willingness of an individual to do something. But this something happens only when it is conditioned by its ability to fulfill some need for the individual. And understanding these individual needs is the success mantra of understanding the process of motivation.

To add dimensions to the needs profile and to facilitate the build-up of organisational perspective, it is necessary here to classify these needs into two categories: organisational and individual. This ensures that individual efforts are regularised, structured and channelised into organisational need fulfillment and hence organisational performance. So, in an organisational perspective, my previous comment on motivation could be modified as an individual's willingness to exert extra efforts for achieving organisational goals, conditioned by this "extra effort's" ability to satisfy individual, personal needs. Inherent in this statement, therefore, is the significance of understanding individual needs.

One of the first attempts to profile individual needs had been done by **Abraham Maslow** in his theory on the hierarchy of human needs. According to him, an individual progresses through **FIVE NEED LEVELS—physiological (relating to his need for food, sex and other basic requirements), safety (relating to his need for shelter, security, etc.), social (the need for friends, family, etc.), esteem (relating to his need for recognition and respect), and finally his self-actualisation reflecting need for achieving greater things.** Does it remind you of the Cake example?? This hierarchy still forms the basic structure for understanding individual needs. To illustrate these five levels and make way for lucid comprehension, I would take you on another guided tour, this time through the life of Hari.

It starts when Hari, a twenty-three-year old unemployed youth, was taking an idle, aimless stroll down the busy circles at Connaught Circus on a crispy autumn morning, cursing his life, the government and scores of others who couldn't make any difference to his existence. There were people racing past him to reach their workplaces on time. Suddenly, a youth clutching a briefcase and running at full speed bumped into Hari. The next moment he saw a suit-clad gentleman running towards him, asking Hari to grab the man with the briefcase. Without wasting a moment Hari nabbed the youth, got the briefcase and handed it over to the gentleman. The gentleman introduced himself as Ronnie, owner of an apparel manufacturing company. He thanked Hari for saving his company from losing a crucial order, as the briefcase had the contract papers apart from the money. He asked Hari whether he could be of any help to Hari. Hari's primary need at that time was something that could secure him two square meals a day—he asked for a job. Ronnie promised him one and asked him to come the next morning to his 10th floor office in

> **Ronnie was impressed at Hari's exemplary motivation. Hari was confirmed in the job six months later**

Connaught Place. The next morning, Hari was offered a peon's position, which he gladly accepted.

Hari started putting in his best for his saviour, cleaning up Ronnie's room every morning and keeping it as tidy as it could be. A week later one morning, Hari found Ronnie restlessly looking for something. On enquiry, he found that Ronnie had forgotten some papers in his car and was wondering how to get them as there was no electricity and hence the lift was not working. On learning about this, without waiting for the lift, Hari dashed down ten floors and got back the papers in a jiffy.

Ronnie was impressed at Hari's exemplary motivation. Hari was confirmed in the job six months later. He was given an appointment contract and was offered the benefits due to him. Days went by. And then one day, Hari paid (a fifteen rupee) membership fee and joined the employees' union. Two days after that Hari was summoned to Ronnie's room; this time he was asked to get Ronnie's mobile phone which he had left in the car. As luck would have had it, there was no electricity too. Surprisingly however, this time Hari refused saying that such activities were not a part of his job responsibilities. Ronnie was taken aback. Hari related this encounter with Ronnie to his canteen and union colleagues and told them how he

*When nothing seems to help,
I go and look at a
stonecutter hammering
away at his rock,
perhaps a hundred times,
without as much as a
crack showing in it.
Yet, at the hundred-and-first
blow it will split in two,
and I know it was not
that blow that did it
but all that had
gone before.*

had refused Ronnie on his face. He was applauded by his colleagues for his brave and rightful response. Now everybody looked up to him. Delirious with his recent popularity, Hari started participating more in union activities and in a short span of time became a hot favourite with his colleagues. He would address the canteen gatherings and would apprise his colleagues of their rights.

One pre-Diwali morning, as Ronnie stepped out of his Mercedes, he was gheraoed by a group of slogan-shouting and placard-touting employees, accussing Ronnie and the management on their employee-apathy and blood-sucking practices. This time Ronnie was not particularly taken aback to discover that the gherao was led by the erstwhile naive, innocent, down-to-earth Hari, the same guy whom he had a chance encounter with

You are not the same person you were ten years ago and you are not likely to be the same person ten years from now

at Connaught Circus. A seasoned manager that he was, he could figure out the changing profile of Hari's individual needs. Without fuming over the new 'avataar' of 'Hari-the-Leader', Ronnie addressed him as a leader, called him over to his personal cabin, sat across over a cup of coffee and some pastries and negotiated with him to sort out the issue. Hari reciprocated the status accorded to him by his saviour and worked towards a win-win solution. Inspite of his revolt, Hari got a promotion. Finally, after many years, he retired from work as the leader of the union. Two years after Hari's retirement, Ronnie received a courier packet one evening at his residence. There was a book inside wrapped with a note—'To Mr. Ronnie—With Warm Regards, Hari'. Ronnie opened the wrapper. It was 'Labour and Management— Practices for Synergy' authored by Hari and dedicated to him!

The brief lifesketch, I hope, has been able to make way for some comprehension on how an individual's needs progress through stages—Hari's need for two square meals a day to his putting in extra efforts to get his job confirmed. Then his need to affiliate with others and his joining the union to his extra efforts towards leading the union followed by his organised movement against Ronnie the owner and the management. Finally his efforts towards structuring his experiences in the book.

Such progressive developments of needs could be experienced by all individuals and hence, as I said earlier, this constitutes the base for understanding individual needs. This approach however, I repeat, should remain as the base for understanding individual needs. More than that is the basic realisation that every individual is a changing entity and there is no conclusive method of doing a final analysis of human needs. I emphasise on this realisation because I find people ordinarily speak of themselves as though the self were a stable and unchanging entity. You are not the same person you were ten years ago and you are not likely to be the same person ten years from now.

All of us while studying imagined how our life would be after college—getting a job, starting an enterprise, getting married, having children, earning more money, going abroad—this was definitely so for the elite group in class. While planning for the future what we always forget to take into account is the fact that we would also keep changing with the years. What I am trying to bringforth is the fact that we all have a self-concept, but we are not also aware of other possible selves as well. By saying so, I reiterate once again that the success mantra for understanding human motivation and motivating others lies, first, in the realisation that, like ourselves, all others also have a self-concept as well as other possible selves. And, second, it is necessary for them to provide for areas and opportunities to fulfill their individual needs and honour their other selves in tandem with the organisational goals.

I would now attempt to lay threadbare the process of need development in an individual. As per this, the process of motivation in an individual starts with an unsatisfied need, anything that he desires but is deprived of. For instance, Hari probably wanted to be treated well and respected in his social group. The fact that he was not initially treated in this way created an unsatisfied need in him. Such deprivation resulted in tension.

Tension, however, should not be referred to in the way it usually is. **In fact, it's tension that drives us towards extra efforts.** Going by this argument, let me state that tension in an individual could have a negative or a positive (meaning a functional or a dysfunctional) manifestation. For a positive performance through a motivated effort, **we need the functional tension which perked up Sergei Bubka year after year to create and relentlessly break previous records in pole-vaulting.** Problems however emerge once this tension takes up a dysfunctional turn. An individual in such a case doesn't get psyched-up towards increased efforts. This leads to poor performance and hence possibly poor rewards resulting in frustration, which at its worst manifestation could lead to aggression in workplace.

Another problem is that of employee indifference. Because of ill-planned reward systems, supervisory goof-ups, etc., an individual gets distanced from the organisation and stops feeling like an insider. This results in an apathetic manifestation in an individual which keeps him away from any tension whatsoever making him indifferent.

I will deal with such problems later. Let me now go back to explaining the process. The process that I would sketch is an adaptation of the widely accepted expectancy theory of motivation. Individuals experiencing functional tension would put in their efforts to fulfill their unsatisfied need. Greater would be the efforts if they would result in some achievements of value to them.

Therefore, you will not disagree if I say that **motivated people are in a constant state of functional tension.**

Please note that what I am implicitly trying to say is that let us create an environment which results in higher tension which in turn would mean more

The normative component is built by allowing individuals to participate more in the matters relating to the organisation

people getting engaged in organisational activities

*At first people
refuse to believe that
a strange new thing
can be done,
then they begin
to think it can't be done.
Then they see it
can be done.
Then it is done
and all the world
wonders why it was
not done before.*

rather than creating an environment of cold apathy with indifferent people, which I have come across in many organisations.

The problem however is that it is easier said than done, because effective motivation would require larger and bigger efforts on our part to put a lot of bits and pieces together and, believe me, it is an unbelievably fragile mass.

This is no reason to despair however, for there are ways, and ways unlimited to get people to do things which would lead to more efforts, or rather extra efforts from their side. This definitely needs a closer understanding of human self and an innovative and determined approach from everyone concerned.

One such approach to psyche people into putting extra efforts is by building organisational commitment. It broadly defines one's attitude towards one's organisation. It refers to the extent to which individuals identify themselves with their organisations, are involved in its activities, and also the extent to which they are unwilling to leave their organisation.

One such attempt to understand organisational commitment has been done by **Meyer and Allen** in 1991. They propose that organisational commitment involves three different components. The first is affective component, referring to the individual's emotional attachment to and his identification with the organisation and its goals. A person high in this component feels proud about his organisation and states with pride that he is a "Tata Man" rather than 'I am working for Tata'. Second is the continuance component, referring to the costs perceived by the individual in discontinuing with his organisation. The third is the normative component, referring to the obligation experienced by an individual towards his organisation because of shared values and norms.

This helps us go closer to an individual's needs profiles and thus could be a good navigator for getting to build organisational commitment. As for the affective component, it can be enhanced by increasing an individual's freedom at work. **Freedom does not necessarily imply compromising on controls.** It could mean some degree of autonomy to an individual to at least structure his work and activities. The affective component could also be increased by designing jobs in such a way that they are skill-enriched. This means an individual works on a job that requires doing a lot of varied activities. This also means that the individual is able to identify himself with a complete piece of work done. This makes individuals relate to the organisation and identify with its activities.

The continuance component is largely a function of the tenure of an individual in an organisation and the long-term benefits that are designed. The normative component is built by allowing individuals to participate more in the matters relating to the organisation. This creates a sense of obligation in the individual towards the organisation and thus the individual starts feeling like an insider.

The question that might be disturbing the mind of the reader is why am I deliberating on organisational commitment to discuss motivation. What I am trying to reach through this is what is called organisational citizenship. **Organisational citizenship** results in an individual making sacrifices for the organisation. The greater the citizenship behaviour, the greater is the willingness of the individual to put in extra efforts for the organisation, engaging more in organisational activities and moving closer towards attuning individual needs with organisational needs and goals. This citizenship behaviour is no doubt a constant source of functional tension to an individual, a concept which I had discussed earlier.

Let me now take up yet another critical issue in motivation—the long debated issue of the money link in motivation. **Money has always been thought of as a great motivator.** However, organisations have started believing that money only constitutes the hygiene factor as per **Frederick Herzberg's** famous two-factor theory of motivation. As per the same, money in itself does not necessarily lead to motivation. Inspite of this, I still find people referring to money, or rather the lack of it, as the reason for general absence of motivation among a lot of organisations.

Money, I would like to say, only denotes the price of an employee. **It is not just money but recognition which is the basic requirement for creating a motivating work culture.** It is recognition which enthuses an employee and provides the functional tension, thereby leading to increased efforts. And by mentioning the money-significance, I just want to emphasise that there are other ways to recognise individuals and their performance. **One such powerful and effective motivator is strokes.** Let us now get some perspective on this.

Every individual, irrespective of whether he is working with a large organisation or with a small one, has **three levels of hunger—status hunger, structure hunger and stroke hunger.** These levels of hunger meet their psycho-social needs and hence provide the drive to put in efforts, or rather extra efforts. Stroke hunger results from the need to be recognised, the need to feel that one exists, the need to feel that one is important. The reader by now must be wondering what strokes actually mean. A stroke, for simplicity, can be defined as an unit of existence. It tells somebody that he exists, that he is needed, that he is being noticed. Stroke is something that we all look forward to from others around us, especially from our leaders, our managers, our mentors. But believe me, it is in unbelievably short supply in this world. We tend to ignore this immensely potent means of motivation by taking people for granted and taking their efforts for granted.

What I want you to realise is that small tokens of appreciation for your people can change the way they look at you, your organisation, or should I say their organisation, the work that they do and the purpose that you both together strive for. All of us need to take such initiatives and make others feel that they exist, that they are important. This would go a long way in creating all the functional tension that I have been talking about, creating a workplace with more Sergei Bubkas and all such people with fire in their bellies...

&

*End note: People are your most
important resource and if the
people you work with can
become your friends they would
be with you even in hell...
helping you taste success.*

TALK MAN
& I CAN
SEE THEE

Talk Man &
I Can See Thee
The Four Principles for
Effective Communication

Anthropologists would have made us believe that there is less than a 2% difference (what they say is DNA) between us and the 'Chimpanzees'. Like it or not, they prove this with research. Well, it's just that we decided to make the best of this difference

----

ARINDAM CHAUDHURI

and went ahead to conceive civilisations and cultures with our "genie" of communication. We went beyond the restrictive hoots and grunts to evolve a system of communication by harnessing the ability to express complex human ideas and develop a far higher level of synergy. From the primitive wheel, to the pyramids, the epics, man's first step on moon and to the genome engineering, mankind has made the best of the 2% bestowed upon us by nature.

Today, however, because of its commonplace nature, communication more often than not gets scant attention and at best enjoys an 'Oh, Well Yes, It's Important!' status. If organisations are all about people and what drives them is people power, then communication should be seen as the powerhouse that generates this people power, so very essential to propel the organisation to its peak performance. Successful leaders have all been great communicators. I remember reading somewhere that Lincoln due to his poverty owned only a few books. Yet, he used to read and reread them till the language of the books became his. And later of course his communication skills made him one of the greatest leaders and communicators of our times.

In fact the only work that we do the entire day, each day of our lives, is to communicate. We communicate verbally and we communicate non-verbally, we communicate within and without and we also communicate with people and with inanimate things around us. In the earlier chapter, we have looked at ways of motivating those around us and the only way to do so is by communicating to them and communicating effectively. So let's get this act straight, let's make the best of communication and continue to revel in the glory of civilisation.

The first principle for effective communication:
Don't forget the LAW i.e. Looks, Actions and Words

Looks

Looks can be killing. I had always believed this statement to be an adage used for handsome-looking hulks and sweet, lovely beauties, but realised it could be used otherwise. I learnt that Prashant Ragavnath (name changed) who was with us in the B-school, a genius of a kind in studies, but not the best person to be sharing a room with, had been given an expulsion notice from an organisation of repute as he failed to comply with the regular "proper bath, shave, clip fingernails, tie knot...." norms of the organisation. Different organisations have different dress codes, and like fads and trends these do change. But our looks do a lot of talking for us since everyone around us is but human and can easily fall into the perception trap.

Hasn't someone said **"God made Adam and Eve but tailors made Gentlemen and Ladies"**. I don't mean that if you are born with Pierce Brosnan's or Aishwarya Rai's looks you are any better communicator, but you sure should have a pleasing, smiling personality which endears you to whom you communicate with. In China you don't open shop if you don't smile. You shouldn't anywhere else either. When I enter my office every morning, I must see a smiling face on each of the 110 MBAs in our office to reassure me that all is fine and business is happening as usual.

Looks are not just about expressions but also about the way one dresses up. It's not just about not going for a funeral service wearing a bright red shirt but also about power-dressing for that important meeting of yours. You look good for your interview and chances are that you will be selected because organisations are looking for impressive surrogates. Apart from a game of chess, where neither your communication skills nor the way you look matters, everywhere else it would.

Actions

Actions speak. Our body language, non-verbal gestures and our mannerisms do a lot of talking for us. I get to watch many a presentation of my students who work very hard for my subject 'National Economic Planning'. My assessments apart, I find the other competing groups having a field time reviewing the presenters' hand movements and body language besides counting the number of times he/she has used the word 'OK'. I learnt later that they had classified one of the presenters as an **"Athlete"** as his hand movements were faster than the speed of his speech; the other as a **"Padre"** as he would speak with folded hands throughout the speech; yet another as a **"Jauhri"** as he would fiddle around with a necklace, key ring and other "jewels" on his person, and finally one as the **"Adam's Figleaf"** as he would keep his hands folded in front of him as if in an attempt to protect an external agency hitting him where it hurts the most.

Have you ever come across a sweet, good-looking receptionist who is answering all your queries with a nice "May I Help You" tag pinned to her dress but you somehow get the feeling that she would rather have you going out as early as possible from the same glass door that you entered. Well, if you have it's nothing new. And if you have not, then recall the last time that you were window-shopping and the counter sales person hounded you with questioning looks trying to size your credit worthiness.

HELP YOUR PEOPLE

Choose a job they love

And they won't need to work for even a day.

A man who does not love his work is losing the best part of his perks.

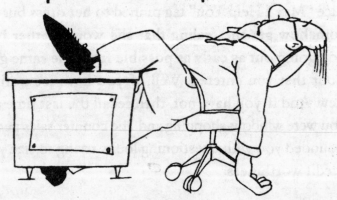

Your lovely and genuine efforts in being nice to your people can be ruined if your actions don't match your words. For example, a good morning wish without a cheerful face doesn't make one feel too good about the morning or for that matter talking to your colleagues without an eye contact (for that matter looking into the ceiling) can make others feel as if you are totally uninvolved.

Most importantly, if you can't display useful actions at least don't display useless actions like sneezing without covering your nose or talking to somebody with your legs up on the table and the shoes facing him.

Watch out for your body movements and gestures as others are watching you.

Perfect actions and body language have always been one of the greatest assets of great communicators. With their hand gestures and perfect expressions they have led their countries out of great miseries. Every time **Fidel Castro** the great leader spoke, he spoke **hands folded in front of him as if in an attempt to protect an external agency hitting him where it hurts the most** for hours. He gave speeches which lasted five hours and millions were enthralled. In United Nations he made history by giving one of his longest ever speeches (it lasted more than three hours). What kept his audience gripped (and often had their blood boiling) was not just what he spoke but also the way he spoke. His posture, his hand movements and expressions have all added up to his immense fan following across continents.

In the same 1960 UN meet, where Castro spoke for three hours (which the press termed as the **"Greatest Show on Earth"**), the then Russian President Nikita Khrushchev also made history for his bold actions. When Harold Macmillan, the British Prime Minister, called for better East and West ties, **Khrushchev angrily banged his shoe** on the Soviet delegation's desk. Did his actions make an impact? You bet, it did. And it was well practiced because the shoe that he banged was probably a spare shoe that he was carrying in his pocket.

It is Castro's actions which even today keep his ardent followers excited. On the day the recent US elections were being held, Castro was seen taking a stroll on the beach in his shorts. When asked by a journalist how come he was so relaxed on such a crucial day, he said that he was doing what most Americans do on that day (American voters just barely manage to have a turnout of 50%). **His actions made a much more powerful statement than his words ever could have.**

This reminds me of the way he had camped out in a Harlem hotel, the Thresa, on 125th street in New York (calling it a show of solidarity with oppressed black Americans) instead of staying in the five star hotel provided for him during the 1960 UN General Assembly! Everybody talks about feelings for the blacks but nobody had done this in past. His actions had won over thousands of American hearts inspite of the differences in ideology.

There are people who at times come to your office, and upon being asked if they would like to have something would say the obvious 'no'. Then you serve them a few snacks. They don't just eat it all up but also leave your room with a few oily finger stains on your most important papers.

Or have you been to a marriage party and witnessed the way people fight with the chicken leg and make a scene out of it?

Did somebody say **"actions speak louder than words"**?

WORDS

"It's only words. And words are all I have to take your heart away". Boy Zone thankfully reminds us of the power within us to be able to become the king of hearts.

In his early 20s, **Karl Marx** said, "We need to bring about changes in the world through violent revolutions." His words stored in the book *Das Capital* were so powerful that it laid the foundation for revolutions in more than 70% of the land mass on this earth. **Words can be powerful.**

If you want to lead a progressive organisation where everyday new ideas are tried and tested, just watch your words. **The right words, however few, could trigger many a brilliant idea, bringing fresh life into your organisation.** It's possible. After all you can count the number of seeds in an apple but you never know how many apples a single seed can bear. So sow seeds of praise, of goodwill, of wisdom and of knowledge around in your organisation and watch your organisation grow and prosper.

"How else would you have known unless I told you".

His actions had won over thousands of American hearts inspite of the differences in ideology.

These few words brought such immense happiness to a colleague who was not particularly happy or sad with his work; when the other, a relatively reserved person, pointed out to him that he was doing a lot of credible work and added the above statement, it propelled him to a higher level of efficiency and the two went on to become a great team.

Words have had the power to change civilisations. History is replete with examples of battles won, Independence achieved, big sacrifices made—all because someone said a few words to make that difference. **Wrong words at the wrong time have been equally catastrophic.** So, watch your words lest you should have to eat them.

Right words are to be said at the right time. No use trying to tell somebody about how careless he is and how he should be careful and so on when a person has just had a bad accident. Some people love calling a spade a spade. My advise to them is don't always call a spade a spade; at times you might just get one on your head.

The second principle for effective communication: Be audience-friendly

A friend of mine on a busy Sunday morning, trying to catch a train from New Delhi, baggage in hand, rushed into the railway station and momentarily paused to ask an idle railway porter "Where is the Shatabadi?" He hurried off in the pointed direction and just about managed to catch the train. After self-complimenting his athletic skills, when, to strike a conversation with a fellow passenger, he inquired the time the train would reach Dehradoon. The expression on the fellow passenger's face said it all. My friend had got on to the Shatabadi which was destined for Lucknow. What had happened was that all the Shatabadis leave the New Delhi junction within less than half an hour of each other's departure for different destinations. My friend had asked for the Shatabadi and the porter had pointed to one which was just leaving. The porter would obviously not bother to inquire for the details. (It should have been vice versa). Ever since, the common joke between us friends is that "look the Shatabadi is coming" whenever we spot this friend of ours. One might call him a fool implying that he is reckless and should plan his schedule etc., but wait "fool" in English dictionary means a clown, a court jester. Maybe the word that we should use is foolhardy. So let's watch out. We ask incomplete questions and we will only get incomplete answers.

Over the years we work hard to improve our vocabulary; every new word learnt adds on to our storehouse of knowledge and information. Such is the power of this learning that it escalates us to great heights and puts us on a platform higher than those around us. From "there" it might be possible that we are heard but not necessarily listened to. Because "here" are the lesser mortals who neither understand our language nor its essence. They stare blankly when we sing "Sintlet Sintlet Globule Vivesic ..... thy nature specific". Haven't they been to kindergarten and was not this the first rhyme they learnt? "Twinkle twinkle little star...". They don't understand that "Residents of vitreous abodes should not hurl lithodical fragments" is one of the most simplest proverbs that they use so often— "Those living in glass houses should not throw stones."

The point in question is not whether they should have known or whether we should have known that they wouldn't know, but the fact that we have created a barrier between us and them which inhibits communication.

Also the power of knowledge might propel us to speak in the finest of details and craft such wordy expressions that our speeches are as long as the Brahmaputra but in reality may lack the kinetic energy. The "Lesser Mortals" get bored with our long speeches. A particular speaker famous for his long speeches started his speech with the usual "Ladies and Gentlemen, I will take 10 minutes of your time. Well, I was wondering where to start from". Much to the organisers' relief, the speaker did not hear a faint voice from amongst the back benches which quipped, "Well start from the 9th minute."

Lest this should ever happen to us, we better follow the KISS (Keep It Short and Simple) principle.

In one of the GOTA (Global Opportunity and Threat Analysis) trips to Switzerland, I entered a shop with a few of my students to buy Swiss watches to take back home as gifts. An energetic salesperson approached us with a nice smile.

I had liked a Swatch watch and he had seen my eye savouring the beautiful piece. He picked it up as one would pick a Kohinoor and placed it on my wrist. Still with smiling eyes he waited patiently till I had my fill and politely answered all my queries pertaining to the watch. I did not bargain on the price. No one bargains on the "Kohinoor". Does anyone? However, I thanked him and thought it is better to look around before buying any 'Kohinoor'.

In the shop across the street, we encountered another energetic salesman who proceeded to show us a "brilliant" watch. He went on to explain the masterpiece that the watch was. The next 20 minutes we were enlightened by the salesperson as to how the watch was the best we could ever think of having, as it was scientific and showed the wind direction, could calculate astronomical figures, receive the FM, with the indiglo dial...

At the end of a wonderful presentation that lasted a good 20 minutes, he asked me what I thought about the watch and if I had any question. I only had one and on being invited asked it right away. "Does the watch show the correct time?" Well it did sound like a joke and the salesman knew that. Thanking him on the pretext of looking around we made a hasty retreat and went back to buy the "Kohinoor" (actually I wanted it for my grandfather who was a rather simple man and believed that our forefathers lived in a better world).

Our speaking styles are different as are our accents. Most often we encounter situations where even with the best of intentions we are not able to communicate to the recipients the essence of our contents, who in turn perceive the communication as entirely different from what we had intended. This reminds me of another interesting incident!

I am not a great tennis fan, so when I heard a young girl in the front row of a bus I was travelling in exclaim to the person sitting next to her "I wonder how at this age Jimmy Connors can do it so well for three hours", I couldn't help myself from secretively wanting to know who this macho man was.

No one bargains on the 'Kohinoor'. Does anyone?

Another day, I was rather confused when a student conducting a marketing research for a particular shampoo apparently believing I would be a good respondent because of my long hair and ponytail asked me "Sir, would you rather not use a non-medicated shampoo?" I still am not very sure about the answer.

I was discussing a restructuring exercise with the "Boss" (Director) of a company when we were interrupted by a loud voice from outside. The General Manager was probably rebuking a lady secretary. "First you lie with the supervisor, then with me and tomorrow you will lie with the boss ...." he went on. I looked up to catch that glint in the boss's eyes which definitely meant that he was toying with a few brilliant ideas.

Once I was introduced in a corporate party to a charming young lady. The host introduced her as a "carrier girl who is the spark plug of the whole organisation". The lady not a trifle bit embarrassed acknowledged my presence and drifted on to greet other guests leaving me rattling my brains. Three hours later by the end of a wonderful party particularly made interesting by the young lady, I realised that my host meant that she was a very "career" oriented girl and that she made things around her and her organisation lot more lively by her presence.

I am sure we all encounter similar incidents where if a wee bit of clarity could be induced it could make a lot of difference in what the people around us perceive.

The third principle for effective communication:
Be polite and polished

As a speaker, we need to know our audience and be empathic and polite to them.

I was travelling to Frankfurt for one of my official visits. I happened to be flying Air India. It so happened that due to bad weather conditions the flight got delayed by 2 hours. Perplexed as to why I was not informed earlier and quite uncertain as to what to do next, I approached a lady behind the Air India counter. Much to my chagrin, I realised that the lady behind the help-desk, quite oblivious to the discomfort of the passengers, sat on her seat in a semi-Natraja position with a "Sarita" in her hand. My query resulted in a blank "what can I do if the monsoons are creating a problem" look. Resigned to my destiny I spent a good four hours stranded at the airport.

In a similar such incident, I was delayed in boarding my flight to Geneva. However, this time I happened to be flying *KLM*. A smart smiling lady standing behind the help-desk comforted me saying that the technical problem resulting in the delay would be soon taken care of and if I could please step into the waiting lounge and relax while *KLM* would be too happy to offer complimentary coffee and magazines. Ever since, I have been flying *KLM* and so have many others but never Air India. Being sincerely tactful, thoughtful and appreciative of the other person and his viewpoint can make all the difference in how we communicate with others and leave behind a lasting impression.

It is generally a better idea to be diplomatic say "as usual the captain was all dignity personified" than to say "the captain was sober today" implying as if other days he isn't. Very often I used to feel my compliments to pretty young ladies were not getting the required response. It's when I started saying "as usual you look very good" instead of "you look good 'today'" that things changed.

One of the most important things in communication is perhaps the fact that, what you talk fades over time but how you felt remains for a long time to come. You might have a wonderful discussion with somebody today, but after a month, what you discussed may not be as clear in your mind and after a year it may almost become vague... but how you felt, the warmth of the feelings exchanged would stay back for long time to come. That's why politeness is such a virtue... It creates lasting impressions.

The fourth principle for effective communication:

Bring in the humorous human touch

As one of my students, whom I met recently during a marriage ceremony, put it when I enquired how his work was, "Sir, one thing I learnt at *IIPM* is that you can take the skin out of the other person; but if you can humour them, they don't even feel bad!". As the Dean of *IIPM*, the task of managing 700 students every year and adhering to rigorous academic schedules as well as discipline levels is a tough task. Believe me, at *IIPM* the definition of cheating during exams includes even asking for a spare pen! And the punishment for any kind of cheating is the paper being torn off. Yet, students never protest. We mix all our strictures with a lot of humour and communicate it humourously. The notice declaring the rules before the examinations begins in a very humourous way citing examples of all possible ways one can cheat. Of course the punishment for all is one line (about the paper being torn off) written in the end. It works.

In my workshops, I tell my participants to use humour effectively. It can also be developed over time even if you are not naturally funny. You don't always need to be naturally funny to have a sense of humour. Have you ever noticed people who don't generally smile much suddenly one day laughing at a joke? The effect is terrific. Our view changes completely and we feel, "after all this fellow does have a sense of humour". Research confirms that managers who use humour in their presentations with employees come across

> **And the punishment for any kind of cheating is the paper being torn off. Yet, students never protest.**

as more approachable and people are more likely to open up with them. If you manage a lot of people, it's easier to maintain morale and enthusiasm by showing you have a good sense of humour.

Robert Half International surveyed Vice-Presidents and Personnel Directors of over 100 largest American corporations. **The results were incredible. 84% thought employees with a sense of humour do a better job than people with little or no sense of humour. Robert Half interpreted the surveys as follows: "People with a sense of humour tend to be more creative, less rigid and more willing to consider and embrace new ideas and methods". A sense of humour might actually give you an edge in your career. A survey done by *Hodge-Cronin and Associates Inc.* of 737 CEOs of large organisations showed that 98% of them would hire a person with a good sense of humour over a person who lacks humour.**

CULTIVATING HUMOUR

There are ways of using humour, which anybody can cultivate. Some of the simpler ways are to use old jokes, quotes, cartoons, analogies, observations, etc. One has to have this never-ending urge to put a punch in the speech. Analyzing your audience well, talking their language, putting a punchline at the end, creating an image around the statement, putting the audience in the picture can all go ahead and make your speech humourous.

Another good way of bringing humour is by **cracking a joke on yourself.** When I ask my students to come well dressed for interviews I also tell them to have a decent hair cut for better impression and not get carried away by my ponytail.

As the CEO, Sandra Kurtzig of *ASK Computer Systems Inc.* describes how she built the $200 million company from scratch, "When I started this company my long-range planning consisted of figuring out where I would go to lunch". The executives of ASK do find her more approachable.

These kind of lines can remove nervousness or fear from the minds of your subordinates.

Then, of course, are some basic rules of being effective with humour. **One should never announce that he is** going to tell a joke. This removes the surprise element that is the heart of most humour. Secondly, it might also increase audience expectations. **Pausing** for the punchline and waiting for the laugh is also a must.

Humour is a terrific **guard against hostility** and difficult situations. My partner, Sandeep, is an expert at it. Being young and conducting training programmes for people, often double our age at times, forces us not to disclose our real age. So once when a CEO insisted on knowing Sandeep's age, he asked back "Which age? The one which I have on my birth certificate, or the one which my mother tells others when she is looking for a suitable match for me, or the one I like telling my workshop participants?".

Remember

Somebody once said, "Verbal communication contributes only 33% to the gamut of communication. The rest 67% is all about listening and no one tells us this better than nature itself. That we have two ears and one mouth probably means that nature meant us to listen twice as much as we speak".

Since the focus throughout in communication is about getting into the other persons' shoes, at Planman we tried to work out a model called the **Communication Behaviour Preference Mapping**. It helped us learn "The Art of Earning Endorsements" and "Comforting Others Through Intelligent Communication". Read on.

Earning endorsements from others is one of the prime challenges that we are faced with everyday, every moment, if that's not an exaggeration. Success largely also depends on our ability to get others to believe in what we believe, and, not only that, to get others to finally do what we want them to do. Earning endorsements from others thus becomes one of the critical factors for our success and effectiveness.

I call it a prime challenge because almost all of us are habituated to 'autobiographical communication'— meaning talking the way we want to talk, behaving the way we want to behave, and thereby, in most of the occasions, imposing our beliefs on others (or at least, that is how others perceive it to be). This results in the creation of an atmosphere of discomfort resulting in disbelief and thereby nullifying our attempts to communicate our views, our thoughts for whatever purpose. All autobiographical

> **Earning endorsements from others is one of the prime challenges that we are faced with everyday**

communication, with a big central 'I', results in turning a blind eye to the needs of the others, making us poor communicators, poor negotiators, poor managers, and poor leaders.

I strongly believe in the fact and it has convincing empirical support too, that to be effective in getting things done, in convincing others, in making others believe in what we believe, we need to learn an easy art of earning endorsements. I call it easy because it does not require any thorough training to learn the skills (though we do it in our training programmes), or a super intelligent analytical mind. It just needs an appreciation of the fact that all of us have our own characteristic communication behaviour preferences and that we need to respect the same.

However, to make things simpler to understand, I would give you a simple framework that we have developed at Planman that would help you in appreciating the same. The framework attempts to categorise the communication behaviour preferences of individuals into four broad types. This typification however is not to restrict your creative thinking on the same, but to facilitate your thoughts to appreciate and respect differences.

The Communication Behaviour Preferences Mapping is based on the categorisation of individual preferences on two key dimensions of communication. We have opted for two dimensions to make things simpler and easy to comprehend. The first dimension is that of **Persuasiveness**—the tendency and ability of individuals to present thoughts in an assertive, convincing manner, often with the use of power of position, expertise, actions, legitimacy or otherwise. Tendency and ability have been considered to include both competency and attitude. The second dimension is that of **Expressiveness**—the tendency and ability to control or express emotions during communication. The dimensions range from high to low and thereby create four distinct styles of communication behaviour preferences. An instrument has been developed to assess and map individual preferences.

I would now explain the four distinct styles with illustrations of some highly visible personalities to help you identify and relate easily to the same. The illustrations however are only for understanding and are based on their public face and thus might not necessarily reflect their characteristic behaviour preferences.

People with **high Persuasiveness and high Expressiveness** are the **Thespians**. My illustration would be of **Bill Clinton**. These people prefer an action-oriented communication liberally using gestures,

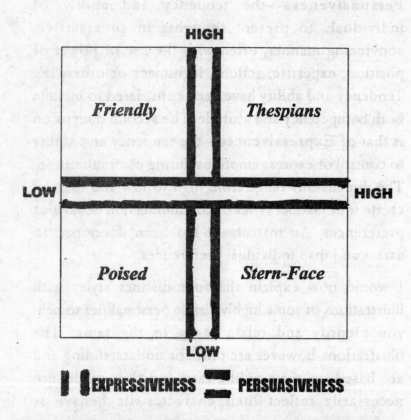

COMMUNICATION BEHAVIOUR PREFERENCE MAPPING

expressions, and movements while communicating. The readers must have observed the expressiveness of Clinton in his numerous TV appearances for varied reasons. These people also have a natural persuasiveness and thus their voice modulation and their stress on the keywords while communicating. They are almost always as convincing as a film or theatre actor and hence the name Thespians. Thespians are also characterised by a preference for an informal way of communication. In business, Thespians prefer first to build relationships and then communicate other considerations.

People with **high Persuasiveness and low Expressiveness** are the **Stern-Face**. My illustration would be of **Karan Thapar** and **T.N.Seshan**. They are characterised by a no-nonsense attitude and in almost all occasions prefer carrying a stern-face while they communicate, and hence the name. One must have observed the way people feel threatened facing Karan Thapar in a TV interview. They usually prefer direct words without considering whether the listener might feel comfortable or not, and prefer

> **They are almost always as convincing as a film or theatre actor and hence the name Thespians**

making hitting statements. I remember Mr. Seshan once replying to a query raised by a journalist on how he would tackle the politicians. His reply was typical of a Stern-Face—"...I will shout. If they don't listen, I will bark. If they still don't listen, I will bite." They might show an indifferent attitude at times and are quite likely to liberally use power as they communicate. In business, the Stern-Face prefers talking straight and strictly about his business and work.

Poised are people with **low Persuasiveness and low Expressiveness**. I would like to present the case of **Amitabh Bachchan** for Poised. Readers should note that I am not referring to the 'Vijay' of Deewar or the 'Vijay Dinanath Chauhan' of Agneepath. I would like to restrict myself to the Bachchan that we see in our TV shows, one who is talking normally to somebody else. These people—please reflect and identify—are poised, calm and are extremely formal. They are careful about the words they use and would generally communicate very slowly. Poised prefer orderliness and seem relatively calm. They are usually formally dressed and have a natural tendency to reflect on issues before commenting. In business, poised are very structured and are usually concerned about talking work.

People with **low Persuasiveness and high Expressiveness** are the **Friendly**. My immediate association with this type is **Pronoy Roy**. The Friendly, as the name suggests, are usually warm in their communication. They are also careful about the words they use to make sure that they don't explicitly threaten others. They usually avoid the use of power in whatever form. You would have noticed how Mr. Roy usually projects a reserved behaviour and avoids any attention-seeking behaviour unlike other TV personalities. The Friendly are also very good listeners, and for this I would like to draw your attention to Mr. Roy's unique style of his fingers on his cheek which is the characteristic body language of good listeners. In business, the Friendly prefer to build relations and not just restrict themselves to work.

I tried my best to make sure that I do not glorify any particular style or denigrate the other. Please note, and this is extremely important, that no style is right or wrong. In fact, this is the central idea of this classification and this would help you to appreciate the differences and respect the same. All people have their characteristic preferences and tendencies and they have been developed over the years through the conditioning, social learning, etc. So I emphasise once again that it is very important to understand and appreciate that all the four styles that I have discussed and the five personalities I have illustrated have excellent communication skills and also that all of them are quite successful in their respective professions or roles.

Now let me get to the most important aspect of the framework—the importance of developing flexibility in earning endorsements. What I mean is that we all need to appreciate that we are most comfortable when others communicate with us in our own preferences. Comfort usually leads to trust and thus makes the attempt to communicate effective. This flexibility can be achieved by 'flexing'; that is, talking to others in their own language. I am sure I need not illustrate the consequences of a communication between two people with their own different characteristic styles. This is what I call a verbal exchange and not communication, because communication intends to achieve more than just a verbal exchange. I remember an instance in an organisation where an employee, who happened to be a thorough Thespian, had to get a sanction from his departmental head, who was a confirmed Stern-Face, for an equipment that required a sizeable investment. It so happened that the fellow, without appreciating and realising, presented the case to his boss in his own characteristic style. His proactive attempt to get that equipment for improving the productivity was seen as an attempt to waste organisational resources by the departmental head. He was, in fact, criticised for his 'undue' consideration. All this just because he failed to understand that the departmental head would appreciate his concern and would sanction the same only when it was presented in a formal, straightforward way. A small ignorance leading to a large consequence. And this is what happens to most of us quite frequently. Don't we complain—'...why the hell that stupid guy doesn't understand this simple logic.' My reply to the same would be 'Have you made an attempt to find out how the 'stupid' guy would like to understand?' That is what is effectiveness, that is how you earn endorsements, that is the heart of the art of comforting others.

Here are some ready references that would help you develop flexibility and aid your 'flexing' attempts. When communicating to the Thespians, don't be too formal. Avoid placing an overemphasis on details of everything. Thespians enjoy speed, and details hamper the same. And do remember to take some time out for socialising. When communicating to the Stern-Face, be direct, specific and to the point. Be formal and present your facts logically. Use figures even if you are emotionally convinced about anything. Remember, you have to convince the Stern-Face. For the Poised, try to be properly organised. The fact of the matter is find out what they appreciate. They would reciprocate nicely if you appreciate their preference for orderliness. While communicating to the Friendly, avoid the use of power. Friendly people get threatened by power. Take time to socialise and to listen to his/her view with attention.

Try this simple exercise. Observe people carefully and try to understand their preferences. Respect their preferences and communicate in their own language. You would observe a significant difference in your communication effectiveness. And yes, also a significant difference in your relationships. Remember, you are comforting others.

> *End note: You can never succeed with people without mutual trust and understanding... Effective communication skills could just be the difference between success and you.*

PEGGING
CULTURAL
HOLES

Pegging cultural holes

Global management practices & Theory 'i' Management

How often has one heard of an American organisation adopting the Japanese management style to surge ahead? How often has one heard of the reverse? Probably never. However, I do remember reading somewhere that when *IBM*-USA was making losses and *IBM*-Japan was making profits, *IBM*-USA tried to adopt the Japanese management style to turnaround. The result was increased losses.

— ARINDAM CHAUDHURI —

Predictable? Should be. So many examples of product failures are there in the world of advertising and marketing with the common reason being failure to adapt with the national culture. The Old Spice advertisement with the focus on a cool feeling excites people in India, India being a hot country. The same is most likely to fail in a cold country like Norway where people long for a warm and comfortable feeling.

It is most likely that a style that is successful in Japan would not be as successful in the US and vice versa.

 *Remember* **People are different, the cultures are different and so is the lifestyle. So management styles also need to be different.**

That is the reason why Japan has developed its own management style and the US its own. For instance, if we take a look into the American management style in general, we realise that it is absolutely finetuned to the American culture and way of living. The people in the West grow up with comparatively less emotional security due to factors like high divorce rates, single parent family, etc. As they grow up they do tend to find a sense of stability in this seemingly unstable and insecure atmosphere. Thus, when they enter into their job-lives and see a management culture prevalent which is contractual in nature with hire-and-fire style of management, they don't get disturbed. In fact, this motivates them to work harder and as a typical American would say "we are tough guys and as long as we are good the company keeps us, else we go out". This statement essentially is a manifestation of an outburst against the accumulated insecurities in their lives. Most of them had their parents asking them to be tough in times of emotional adversities. So, they have grown up trying to convince themselves that they are tough and nothing affects them. Most of the stories of successful corporate turnarounds in the West are based upon

> **As they grow up they do tend to find a sense of stability in this seemingly unstable and insecure atmosphere**

massive retrenchments, reconfirming the fact that hire-and-fire system of management reigns supreme. I call this the **Contractual Style...** on the job as well as back at home. On the job, as **Lee Iacoca** pointed out in his best-selling book: *An Autobiography by Lee Iacoca*, one could be fired because the boss doesn't like the shape of the employee's nose or the style of his trouser. And on the personal front at home your spouse could be fighting a divorce case because you snore in the night; essentially, both the reasons of getting fired and getting divorced are immensely similar (the levels of job insecurity as well as the high divorce rates to make a point). I don't want to question the morality of such management culture, all I want to highlight is the fact that even today more than 50% of the Fortune 500 Companies are American companies.

The bottom line, thus, is that the fine tuning between the general national culture affecting people at home and the management culture affecting people on the job works wonders and enhances productivity and motivation.

However, to confirm this fact we need to look into a few more cases. So, we will look into two more cases of managerial success. First, we will take a look into the more talked about Japanese and the South-East Asian success stories and then we will talk about the Red success (symbolising the erstwhile USSR, East European countries and the current China syndrome). I know the latter is subject to a lot of debate and I am going to justify their inclusion before talking about their styles.

India and Japan started their modern development process more or less at the same point of time. While, India got its independence in 1947, Japan also started its development process around that time too, after being devastated in the Second World War. Both the countries needed to develop fast due to their own respective problems. India was full of potential but left totally empty and exploited by the British, while the Japanese were leaders in their own rights but bombed and left completely shattered by the inhuman brutality of greedy capitalist vested interests. Both the nations in their efforts to grow fast undertook two opposite paths. While the Indians (full of a typical West complex) decided to follow the western style of management; the Japanese decided otherwise. The Japanese looked into their national culture and thought it appropriate to develop their own style of management and its principles. They realised that Japan stood for pretty much the opposite of all that the wild West symbolised. If the West believed in nuclear families the Japanese (then) believed in joint families with immense bonds and respect for each other, if the West believed in hire-and-fire as a way of management, the Japanese employees were looking forward to a more stable atmosphere on the job. Of course, unlike India, the West and the Japanese had one thing in common, they were both hard working and patriotic.

Looking at Japanese companies, one finds concepts of lifetime employment working wonders out there. A Japanese finds the bonded culture in his organisation, unlike the American contract culture. If we look into the Japanese lifestyle and culture we would find the importance of **Bonding** being very high. Those familiar with stories about Japanese families would know that the respect for their elders is unmatched and they are taken care of with utmost affection till the end of their lives.

A 45-year-old man in the family makes it a point to consult his 75-year-old mother very often even for the minutest of decisions he takes in life or work. In India, we had the opportunity for a few months to view the teleserial "Oshin" based on the true story of a Japanese woman, which highlighted Japanese family culture. Sadly, the serial ran out of sponsors, inspite of being an excellent show.

> **If the West believed in nuclear families, the Japanese (then) believed in joint families with immense bonding**

Most probably companies having the ability to sponsor did not like the dignified and moral lifestyle that was being projected since their profitabilities are directly proportional to the consumerist instincts prevailing in the economy. Therefore, these companies are game about sponsoring serials like "Bold & Beautiful" since they project the 'Banana Republic' lifestyle full of glamour, lifestyle products, girlfriends and boyfriends, extramarital affairs and big cars. These serials have

If in the recent past you

haven't DISCARDED one

of your favourite ideas or

ACCEPTED a new one

CHECK YOUR PULSE;

YOU MIGHT BE DEAD

the right mixture to drive in inferiority complexes within people which is necessary for a consumerist society which keeps craving for more and for a better comparative lifestyle.

However, coming back to the main point, the Japanese have strong family ties and a strong sense of community. From such an upbringing, they feel at home when they see a bonded style of management on the job. As I have already mentioned earlier, the typical Japanese would say "I am a Honda man (and not that I work for Honda)" displaying the bond that he shares with his company. If one reads the evergreen book *Made in Japan* by Akio Morita he would realise that the Japanese success is not due to concepts like Kaizen, Zero Defect or Just In Time Management only. Although these concepts might have originated in Japan, the rest of the world has been able to adopt these, as it had little to do with human behaviour. Thus, advantages arising out of such concepts have had a global impact.

If we look deeply we would find that the Japanese miracle was due to nothing but a **fine blend of exceptional micro level management supported by macro level government policies** and commitment. Three main factors that emerge out are patriotism, lifetime employment and wage structure. All these surprisingly are very nicely interrelated.

Patriotism works at a micro level with the Japanese employers; they believe it is their prime duty to keep their entire work force intact. They would rather commit Hara-Kiri (suicide) if they fail to do so. At a macro level the Ministry of Trade and Industry (MITI) sees to it that Japan is not exploited by other countries, thus giving rise to the concept widely known as Japan Incorporated. The States ensured that there was a well-distributed national growth in purchasing power of the masses along with economic growth. This in turn kept expanding the domestic market. Added to this was the emphasis on domestic competition as a matter of macro policy in order to produce quality products which later helped them capture international markets (pretty much the opposite of what we did!).

When a man runs short of money in the market place and goes to borrow some from the policeman round the corner, he meets with a pleasant experience. The policeman might not even ask for his address, for, trust is too high and he knows that a Japanese would never cheat his country. When this is how a citizen is treated, in turn he also acts responsibly and reacts by picking up a waste paper lying by the road and taking it home to throw it in his dustbin.

If all this is analysed properly, we find that it all comes from patriotism at macro as well as micro level. Since

> **when the company is in trouble it can become very flexible by cutting down on bonus which is 80% of total cost**

the Japanese try to survive with their people they very often keep a wage structure such that 20% of it is wages and 80% bonus (this wage structure is approved and supported by the government through suitable policies).

In the peak times the workers get very high, as much as 80% bonus. In the periods when the company is in trouble, it can become very flexible by cutting down on bonus which is 80% of total cost, and thus cuts down the major component of cost—wages to a large extent. This helps them survive in these phases.

Since companies try to survive with their people, they also have the concept of lifetime employment. To stick to this till the last they've another concept i.e. exchange of employees. When a company is going through a bad phase, it gives its labour (surplus) to a company going through a good phase at half rates and pays the other half of the salary from their own account. So, what happens is in a bad phase they can quickly recover by cutting down on cost and the company going through a good phase can make its position better when it gets labour at half the market price, thereby increasing its production and profitability.

For example, if the electronics industry is going through a downturn, *Sony* could lend its workers to *Yamaha* in case the automobile industry is on an upswing. This would enable *Sony* to face its crisis with may be 50% or 75% less costs on one of its main cost components, i.e. labour, and enable *Yamaha* to get labour (again one of the main requisites) at 75% of the market price. In any case, the Japanese believe in giving on the job training to their people more than getting trained people. As Morita points out that unlike Americans who prefer building their walls with bricks, Japanese prefer building their wall with stones. Basically, pointing out to the fact that while the Americans expect their people to be of particular dimensions and expertise (this brick phenomena is today felt to such an extreme extent that some companies reject your application just on the basis of a computerised handwriting test which tells that you are not fit for the job), the Japanese prefer taking them as they are (the stone phenomena: of accepting people the way they are instead of expecting them to have similar qualities) and giving them necessary training programmes whenever they need to upgrade their skills.

The story behind the success of Japan is interlinked between patriotism, lifetime employment and the wage structure. In Japan, we find a socialistic approach with proper planning through **MITI** (though they prefer calling themselves an egalitarian state). The World Bank too has clearly said that whenever companies have intercorporate planning they do well. The whole system is about working in cooperation with each other in a bonded manner.

The point that gets highlighted again is that a management style which flows out of your own culture and roots would any day motivate your people much more than one which is adopted from somewhere else.

Let's now take a look at an extreme example before looking into the Indian case. Many people doubt the success story of the erstwhile communist countries. But perhaps, they should be reminded of the times when the Americans were about to send the first man ever to space. They came to know that the Russians were planning it a few days before them. The rest is history.

Yuri Gagarin became the first man ever in space. It was a moment of national shame for the Americans. The then American President Kennedy came on television and told the nation that an American would be the first man on moon before the turn of the decade. We all know that **Neil Armstrong** became the first man on moon but what we don't know is that just a few days before the Americans were to leave for the moon, the Russians had left for the moon but like other stories of unsuccessful missions to the moon this rocket failed in its mission. However, the Russians did send an unmanned jeep to the moon which took better pictures of the moon.

The point that I am trying to highlight is that not only were the Russians as good technologically but even their intelligence machinery was far superior, so that each time they could time their departures just a few days ahead of the Americans.

Isn't it an irony that even sane men of high repute actually think that the Russians were not capable of producing high quality consumer goods? It was not so. They simply did not do it because at that point of time their emphasis was on global peace and the post second world war history is a proof to the fact that till Russia reigned we had more peace in this world than the post 1990 period. After achieving military equality it was time for the Russians to emphasise on consumer goods but sadly Gorbachev could not manage and implement his wonderful ideas of Perestroika.

The CIA as well as Gorbachev admitted that the Russian per capita income in 1990 was about 40% of that of the Americans. This meant that if Americans at that time were having a per capita income of $15000 the

Even sane men of high repute actually think that the Russians were not capable of producing high quality consumer goods

Russians were at $6000. Compare to the fact that we were somewhere below $200, I am sure I am justified enough in taking the Russian case as one of success. However, if the doubts still persist, the Chinese case will remove all of it.

China did everything right that the Russians could not, specially the liberalisation part. In 1960, **Mao** asked **Stalin** to share his Nuclear secrets. Stalin declined and by 1964 the Chinese blasted their first Nuclear Bomb. Today, if one was to go through the streets of Geneva or Amsterdam or New York, one would observe just one common fact and that is that all the shops on the streets of the West, mostly keep things which are made in China.

From 'high cost high quality' products to 'low cost high quality' products everything is made in China. From the designer items in GAP to Versache, everything is made in China. 'Made in China', today, is a bigger syndrome than 'Made in Japan' was.

The media being owned by capitalists don't like highlighting socialist success stories for their own reasons. Today, China scoffs at American dictates since

America is more dependent on China (for the growing Chinese market) than vice versa. The Chinese have a $20 billion trade surplus with the Americans. China today talks of manufacturing a Chinese Benz and a Chinese Coke. The world takes it seriously. Weren't the Korean companies nowhere just a few years back?

The success story being clarified, let's take a look into the management style behind their success. We find that their success is mainly due to a complete **dictatorial** and **totalitarian** rule which prevailed not only in organisations but in almost every aspect of a man's daily life. Thus, if in the wild West they have **contract** culture; in the far East they have **bonded** culture; in the red world the prevalent culture is of **forced**. In China, at one point of time, bells would go off on street corners at 5 a.m. in the morning signifying that its time to get up and get working.

In Russia one could not criticise the party leaders even in the privacy of their home for one never knew if the spouse is a KGB agent or not. The same atmosphere prevailed on the job, one of total discipline and brutal force. But did I not tell that I am not going to question the morality behind managerial success? All I want to highlight is the fact that the national culture and the management culture had always been finely tuned. It was a forced culture, whether on the job or at home.

The best of Ballet dancers in the Russian Bolshoi troupe would look like rubber dolls without human emotions, and at the first opportunity they run away from Russia. This happened because even something like dancing was a part of the regimentation. After being exploited for years, perhaps, the people did not mind the forced culture as long as they were getting a better living. But the success story essentially is again about having a management style in tune with the prevalent culture.

BASICS OF "THEORY 'i' MANAGEMENT"

Like Theory 'X' which tried to define a worker in its own manner as a mindless lazy rascal who loves shirking responsibilities and the Theory "Y" which tried to define the worker as an ambitious responsible citizen looking for the right environment to contribute constructively, Theory 'i' is an attempt to understand and define the Indian worker just like the Japanese had tried to do with their Theory "Z".

Inspite of India having some of the best management schools of the world and the best reservoir of skilled human talent, our organisations have not been able to do well. Amongst other reasons, one of the most important reasons for the failure of Indian management has been our failure to develop an indigenous management style, which revolves around our cultural

Change is what keeps

us fresh and innovative.

Change is what keeps

us from getting stale.

Change is what

keeps us young.

roots and upbringing. Well-known Indian management institutes have not been able to come out of the various complexes that they suffer from. They are proud that their faculty got trained from an American institute and so on. Nobody says that their faculty has done

> **Theory 'i' is an attempt to understand and define the Indian worker just like the Japanese had tried to do with their Theory "Z"**

research on Indian management and is trying to find out what is good for Indian corporates.

An Indian grows up in a system, where family ties and a sense of belongingness gets absolute top priority.

Coming from an environment of strong family ties, the Indian youngster gets a shock when he sees the job environment practising management philosophies with which he cannot identify at all. There are three typical cases. Two are commonly occurring extremes and well reported, while the third is talked about and rare. The two most common extremes are either around the practice of American philosophies of contractual style of management in most of the private sector organisations or that of lifetime employment in the public sector organisations. Let's take a look at each one.

The American system for obvious reasons is a total misfit amongst the bond-loving Indians. A recent research done on successful Indians in America goes on to prove that successful Indians in America are not necessarily the happiest people. The job insecurities are too high and so are the pressures. The 40,000 odd people who have been forced to come back to India after the IT meltdown is a case in point. Thanks to the dot com era, many Indians today would identify easily with what I am trying to say. In the middle of your career you get lured away by a big package and you wake up a few mornings later to realise that the job is not there. You have got children to support, loans to pay... and your organisation doesn't care!

The other extreme is the lifetime employment ideology followed by the public sector... Not because of any culture-centric idea but because of the socialist ethics of the Nehru era. Though I mentioned in the last paragraph about Indians loving bonds, yet, we are different from the Japanese. They love bonds and they are hard working. When they get lifetime employment, they find ways to repay the company back: in terms of commitment and hard work. We are different. We love bonds but are complacent (refer to the principles of

FORCED   CONTRACT

BONDED   ????!!!

Theory **i**

Management

"Theory 'i' Management"). So, lifetime employment gives us the opportunity to get paid without working. The environment is just not motivating enough to drive people to higher levels of efforts, since it is not backed up by any patriotic instinct or a leader-driven vision.

The third situation—the rare one—is where a few small and a handful of big companies have tried to strike a balance. These are the organisations which have Indianised their practices (I know of some public sector initiatives too, in this direction) to suit the Indian psyche. They knowingly or unknowingly already do the things which make "Theory 'i' Management". The sad part is that sitting in India I know so well about the way *Intel*, *Microsoft*, *IBM* etc. are managed; since the Americans have written about them... they love "theoretising their practices". Thus, we have records of the best practices in America. In India we don't write. There are no best practice manuals. So unless and until one actually works with the *Tatas* or the *Sahara India Pariwar*, one does not realise their values and India-centric management practices. Yet, these organisations are a boon for Indians. Amongst other things in my mind is also the urge to take out a best practice manual very soon.

> **I would even go up to the extent of suggesting that professional studies could be made a part of on-the-job training**

ARINDAM CHAUDHURI

I am a firm believer of theoretising practices for the benefit of everyone. I hate to hear the phrase "Oh! that's theory" because I believe that there is nothing more practical than a good theory. And if your theory is not practical you need to change it and theoretise what is practical. I try to constantly do that.

If we were to ignore the last case, as being rare then what we find is a situation of cultural mismatch. The Indian worker is not able to adjust productively to this cultural mismatch and thus, very often, fails to be as productive as his Japanese or American counterpart.

An Indian worker is perhaps looking at a system of friendly management practices with moderate job security. Instead of the system (specially in PSUs) giving them near 100% job security, it could give them some fear of job security, since Indians culturally like to take life easy and tend to become complacent. While the job security aspect could be reduced, the human touch in managing them could be increased.

Indian workers should be made to feel that the company cares for them through regular training programmes, family welfare schemes, etc. They should be made to feel that they matter in the organisation through programmes which involve them directly or indirectly in various decision-making processes. This would increase their level of commitment for the organisations and perhaps tomorrow we would also see people telling that "I am a Bajaj man" instead of "I am working for Bajaj scooters".

In one of my workshops Senior Manager, Corporate Planning, *NTPC*, P. Purukayastha, could not agree more and cited two beautiful examples. The first related to *NTPC* spending up to Rs. 5 crores on the medical expenses in US for one of its drivers and his wife who were affected by incurable diseases. This incident of humanity has been a motivating factor for all employees for years. The second related to his own experience where he made flexitiming for one of his workers whose wife was ill. This not only removed the troubled look from his face but made him one of the most motivated and committed workers who was always ready to give more than 100% to his job once his wife became well. These two incidents can explain how human touch can do wonders on an average Indian psyche.

I would even go up to the extent of suggesting that professional studies could be made a part of on the job training like in Japan and not that people first get trained and then wander around for jobs like in the US. It has to be kept in mind that Japan without a single business school of repute has produced some of the most successful corporations in the last 50 years, while with so many reputed management schools the US has not been able to stop the entry of one after another of the Japanese organisations into the Fortune 500 list.

Again, I add that Mr. Purukayastha himself went through a training programme after which the company, based upon the results of the test, decided to shift him from industrial relations to corporate planning which has been one of the most motivating aspects of his job.

The idea that I want to suggest is that it is high time Indian companies thought sincerely about their people and develop **"Indian-people-friendly management"** practices. They might have some American touch or some Japanese touch but the thought essentially has to be given on what will suit the Indians. The sad part as I mentioned earlier is that successful Indian managers who have developed indigenous styles of management don't end up theoretising their styles and propagating them through books or articles. In the US almost every semi-successful manager ends up writing a book, and thus today one knows how *DELL* is managed, but one doesn't know how an Indian corporation like, may be, the *Reliance Group* is managed. So, when it comes to learning management the only option is to refer to foreign books and learn foreign management styles.

What is necessary is to develop an India-centric approach to managing people (which needs research as well as inputs from existing good practices). For that, we first need to identify the key character traits of Indians and then depending upon the situation deal with these characteristics in the best possible manner. The following pages are an effort in that direction.

Principles of "Theory 'i' Management"

☞ **Most Indians value emotional bonds and long term relationships.**

☞ **Most Indians value growth opportunities and commitment.**

☞ **Our cultural roots (of tolerance etc.) often make us complacent.**

☞ **Lack of patriotism at a macro level leaves us aimless.**

WHAT DO THESE PRINCIPLES PROVE ?

These principles have been arrived at after a thorough research that we conducted on more than 3000 managers across the country. The managers were asked to talk about their colleagues across functions and levels. The most important revelation from this survey is about the uniqueness of today's Indian psyche. On one hand as expected, the first two points go on to prove our cultural values and a lot of similarities can be drawn with the Japanese value systems. These are values to be appreciated and admired. These values coupled up with hard-working patriotic instincts is what made today's Japan.

Unfortunately, for us, on the other hand, two more character traits (not found amongst the Japanese) also emerged. This is what makes it difficult for us to copy the Japanese style of management and makes the need for an India-centric management approach very necessary.

Every time I go abroad to take a workshop or a seminar... I conduct an exercise. I ask the international participants about how many of them like the Japanese, and hardly any hands go up. I ask them about how many of them like the Americans and I find many hands going up (Americans are traditionally supposed to be the friendly guys). Then I ask them about how many of them like Indians and not to my surprise again many hands go up. Upon being asked the reason for their liking, they have many things to state. Some had had an experience with an Indian subordinate while somebody came to India and found Indians very hospitable. Someone else finds Indians warm, friendly and open... the reasons go on.

I reverse the question, and ask them about how many like the Japanese products, the American products and the Indian products. For the first two a lot of hands go up as expected; but for the last one, rarely I find any hands going up!

This exercise typically explains the Indians... the first part explains the first two principles of "Theory 'i' Management" while the last part, perhaps, explains the last two principles of "Theory 'i' Management"!

When faced with the fact that everything Indian is so cool outside India, Bhangra and Indipop find place in the US pop charts, the global IT revolution has been fuelled by home-grown geeks, in Ohio the Wright State University College of Business and Administration gets renamed after an NRI businessman, our B-school graduates are becoming global leaders, NASA has top Indian scientists, yet Indians have time and again failed to perform in India.

Indians like to blame it on complacency, a characteristic that they like attributing to our culture! It seems Indians look for the first opportunity to become complacent; something that they are unable to become in the Western world of competition and hire-and-fire system. **Complacency in my opinion is the biggest problem in India.** In China, if they find a city or a port attracting international traffic... in no time they change the entire look of the city with well-built roads, highways and infrastructure to be more attractive. Today, if one stands on a Chinese highway, he actually gets confused whether he is in America or China. That's a non-complacent attitude for you! And you bet it attracts FDI! The *Electrolux* CEO tells me that the amount of damage his products suffers while being transferred from Agra to Chennai via Indian roads don't allow him to give the kind of guarantees that he could perhaps give in China, thanks to their terrific infrastructure.

In India we start by setting up a committee! We are almost like the typical cow that sits on the Indian roads unfazed by the traffic around. When somebody gets down and gives it a kick... it still doesn't evoke a strong reaction. We can chop a woman into pieces and throw her into a Tandoor yet the nation would sit quiet. A few women's organisations might move a little like the cow does, when it gets the kick—but nothing happens.

A practically defunct judiciary, an advertising and PR consideration driven press does its best to make things worse in case anybody has any excitement left. And more often than not, 20 years and a small 17th page left hand bottom corner article (about the criminal being set free due to lack of witness), later the same Tandoor chap is the man whom we vote for during the elections.

Not only this, when faced with the question about the lack of patriotic instincts (the research shows that we Indians, ourselves feel that if we were to be bombed the way Japan was, we would still not have worked as patriotically to build our nation) and decaying values; they love to blame it on their leaders.

If our Prime Minister can be bribed Rs 1 crore by a stockbroker, what's wrong in a common man taking bribe; and if a General Manager can take bribe from the company's travel agent; what's wrong if a lower-level employee get some account through corrupt practices? One might argue that even in Japan there is corruption. The reality however is that, in Japan corruption doesn't touch everyday human existence the way it does in India and moreover they have a more effective judicial system from which even their Presidents can't escape. I read that in Uttar Pradesh the fire brigade has started to ask for bribes before starting to put off the fire! Criminalisation of daily life has gone to such an extent that every individual is actually being turned into a criminal.

The socio-cultural and geopolitical environment in India has today resulted in a mixed breed of Indians, who on one hand retain family values and a longing for emotional touch and on the other hand are complacent (given the first opportunity to be) and unashamed of being morally bankrupt. Complacency and moral degradation leads us to do non-patriotic things, even without realising it.

Thus, to make Indians productive, the Indian corporate sector needs an India-centric management theory.

The last chapter is devoted to some of these India-centric management practices and an action plan for Indian corporates. Though the focus is on India, yet I would like to state that **these practices have high degree of global relevance**. The leadership principles can be applied worldwide including the developed countries of the world as well. As I study global management problems, I come to know that in African countries there is a big problem of complacency as well as a law-and-order crisis. Most underdeveloped countries would thus, hopefully have lots of lessons in store too.

> ***End note:*** *Management is about understanding your men. It is about understanding their cultural upbringing and finding out a style to suit the same in order to make them more productive.*

Sleepy Cows To Galloping Horses

Things don't turn

up in this world

until somebody

turns them up

Sleepy Cows to Galloping Horses

Lord Krishna, Mahatma Gandhi & globally relevant Indian management mantras

The problem is to turn sleepy cows into galloping horses. How do we do it? For this I have taken a look into the whole problem at two levels. I firmly believe that there are two ways of making people work. The best way, of course, is to make them work through self-realisation and motivation. But at times when that fails you need to have the right kind of laws and regulations. For example, it's important to educate people about the need to respect women, yet when someone doesn't, it's equally important to have a punishment system which functions (unlike in India) which would immediately take the person to task. The point is to be moral by choice, else be moral due to the fear of punishment.

Thus Theory 'i' Management prescribes solutions at two levels: The Macro & The Micro.

Macro Aspects of Theory 'i' Management

At a macro level, the government and the industry need to set leadership standards that can be looked up to, in order to drive a sense of patriotism and commitment to the country. This can only come through humane and caring policies for the upliftment of the masses implemented with equal zeal, honesty and earnestness.

Firstly and most importantly, we need to realise that the success of our industries or their respective companies does not entirely depend upon the kind of business strategies they have, or the latest jargons that they adopt from their multinational consulting firms, or on their exciting marketing and sales promotional schemes.

The success of Indian companies in the long run depends upon the size of the market that the economy has been able to give them and on the PURCHASING POWER of the people in the country.

The people at the bottom level today need to be given a higher purchasing power along with better health and education facilities which would not only make a huge difference in the quality of human capital in the country but would also satisfy the most important criteria for the growth of the Indian industry, i.e. they would become a part of the consuming market. The market will no longer comprise of 50 million people but of 1 billion people, because it is purchasing power and only purchasing power of the people that determines the long-run growth of any economy, industry and company.

No marketing strategy certainly can achieve the above market expansion. This is pure economics and no miracle. So, not only for the sake of humanity but also for the sake of their own long-run interests, they should support policies which benefit the weaker

There are three types of
executives in the world.
There are those who can get
short term results
and haven't a clue
where they're going to take the
company in the future.
Conversely, there are those
who have a great ten - year plan
but are going to be out
of business in ten months.
And then there are those who can get
short term results in conjunction
with a VISION for the future.
THESE ARE THE LEADERS.
But they are in unbelievably
short supply.

sections of society and contribute towards its success. Countries which are developed today had all taken care of this basic thing before they surged forward.

Ever wondered why inspite of being the world's largest democracy and a liberalised economy, we get less than one-twentieth of the FDI that China gets inspite of China being amongst the world's largest dictatorships as well as a totally controlled market?

The same America which keeps protesting about the Chinese human rights violation all the time sends the maximum FDI to China! Because the rules of the free market leads us to countries which have purchasing power. Because that is where products will sell.

If you need to see success in a liberalised world, then know the basic rules at least!! Recently, the World Bank said that in recorded history, no other country has been able to pull up more number of people from below the poverty line as China has in the last twenty years. The figure they say is 170 million. Add to that my belief that whenever the World Bank says anything good about China, I am sure it underplays it!! So if a country has got the purchasing power ten times more than the number of people, it will get ten times more FDI since chances of the MNC products selling more is ten times more in that country (specially when the populations of the two countries in question are more or less the same).

In one of my interactions with Mr. Teruo Ishii, Managing Director, *Sony*, he agreed to the fact that in China they do more than 10 times the business that they do in India. They definitely are no exception; it is the same with many other organisations.

In my workshops for the last 5 years, I have been talking about the potential Chinese threat and requesting the corporate sector to wake up and take to the government a delegation lobbying for the right issues. But they preferred to lobby for short-term issues and then cried hoarse when the Chinese threat blasted on their faces recently. The need is to act right and fast instead of crying when faced with a difficult situation.

On the highways in countries like Germany, they indicate two kilometers in advance that a speed breaker is ahead; on the highways of countries like Argentina the same notice is just before the speed breaker. In India, we go over a horrible bump and then somewhere we read "what you just bumped over was a speed breaker".

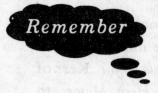

Secondly, and as importantly, we need to have macro-level policies for enhancing the patriotic instincts and the moral values of our country men.

Many people have addressed this problem without ever offering an effective solution. I don't want to commit the same mistake. I believe that an honest and clean macro environment is the most effective solution for this problem. And for this we require to completely revamp our ineffective and lethargic judicial system which for all practical purposes is on a perpetual strike.

Akio Morita in his book _Made In Japan_ devoted a whole chapter on the judicial machinery of Japan, citing that as one of the most critical reasons for the faster growth of Japanese organisations compared to the American organisations (which are perpetually facing legal problems from competitors and customers) during the 70s and 80s. Isn't it amazing that the world's strongest democracy with one of the best judicial systems could be held responsible for American corporate problems by none other than a man of Akio Morita's stature?

In my workshops I interact with top CEOs of Indian companies, and when I ask them about the single most important thing that they look for in their employees... the answer is the same nine out of ten times. From Aquil Busrail of *Motorola* to S.K.Kerr of *HPCL*, from Pankaj Munjal of *Hero Motors* to S. Ganapathy of *Tata Chemicals*, they all vociferously emphasise on **uncompromising integrity**. Obviously the extra emphasis is due to the astounding lack of it. For this I don't blame the moral standards of Indians. I believe, given a chance, anybody from any country would behave like we do, given the present state of judicial system in our country.

Let's take a look at the Indian judicial system to understand the problem better. We have in India 10 judges to every million people compared to more than 120 in the US. In a recent survey conducted, it has been found out that the total backlog of court cases in India is more than 30 million, and on an average it takes 20 years for a dispute to be resolved.

But, of course, disputes being resolved don't mean justice being done. For more often than not the criminal goes scot-free, and justice delayed in any case is justice denied. If this sounds oft repeated, imagine this...

The provincial armed constabulary of UP stopped the buses which were travelling to Delhi to demand a separate state for Uttarkhand. The bus in which the

The world stands aside to let pass the man who knows where he is going.

women were travelling was isolated, the women dragged out, clothes torn and according to the CBI at least seven raped by the 'gentlemen' in uniforms. The menfolk tried to intervene and 14 were shot dead on the spot. The DM of Muzzafarnagar (where the incident took place) said that when a man sees a woman in a deserted sugarcane field the first instinct to surface is the basic desire for conjugal union. Such was his ability to deal with human sentiments as an IAS officer!

At the pace at which our court cases are resolved, it will take another 324 years only to dispose off the backlog. The government is involved in more than 60% of all civil suit appeals. The success rate is often as low as 5% to 6%. It's common knowledge that a large percentage of public prosecutors are on sale. How else can one explain the dismal performance of the government in its own cases. The sad part is that it seems to be a vicious circle—this type of a judicial system benefits the criminals and sends a good proportion of our MPs and MLAs with criminal records to our parliaments, who in turn don't want to change the system.

We are into the Guinness Book of Records not because of big achievements but mostly because of aboriginal habits like the longest nail or the longest moustache or in this case for the longest legal dispute in history. A land dispute in Maharashtra lasted 650 years. All stemming out of what I call the great Indian complacency. Interestingly, most of the chief justices of the supreme court of India know this and generally begin their job by promising to do something about it. But they come and they go, cases keep piling up and criminals keep thriving.

Remember **The reason behind today's moral bankruptcy of the Indians is the lack of trust on the judicial system.**

One prefers to pay a bribe and get the job done, instead of dragging the bribe-seeker to the court. A person does this because he knows that the court will take 20 years to decide his case and in all probability the guilty will not be punished. He thus looks at the option of going to the court as self-harassment. If the case could be solved in three months' time, like it happens in most of the developed countries then he would actually go to court. Even if someone is not punished and given the benefit of doubt- he wouldn't repeat his crime too often. Probably in 9 months to a year's time he would find himself behind bars, for somebody else would also develop the guts to go to the court and finally get him punished.

Thus, to finish this problem of criminalisation and moral bankruptcy from its root, we need to see to it that the judicial machinery starts working and, ideally speaking, we don't have too much time for that. We should try to solve it in the next 5 years itself.

Our research points out that for this we need to allocate Rs. 3,600 crores per year over the next 5 years for employing on emergency services and short service commission, practising lawyers with 5 years experience to act as judges (45,000 additional judges on the basis of Rs. 4 lakhs per judge with supporting staff, etc.) to clear backlog in the next 5 years. Later, as the backlog comes down, these judges would be crucial in keeping up the fast pace of the judicial system. This will reduce criminalisation of civil life enormously and bring back values into our lives and our work.

To achieve the above, we require greater corporate participation in influencing the macro-level decisions through organisations like *FICCI*, *CII*, etc. **pressurising the Government to eliminate poverty,** if not for the sake of humanity then for the sake of their own selfish gains and bringing in a functional judicial system. No amount of management and marketing techniques can enable corporates to have more than 10 to 15% growth in their market nor any amount of moral lectures can make people ethical. But the market can be expanded by more than 1000% by increasing the purchasing power of the people (then, instead of the middle-class being an approximate 50 million it would become more than 550 million) and people can be made ethical through a disciplined judicial system, for without an appropriate punishment mechanism the devil rules our minds as well as our country.

> Show me a country, a company, or an organisation that is doing well and I'll show you a good LEADER

These things I talk about are essentially practices which globally successful countries realised and worked upon. Sadly, these are assumed to be so basic in nature that nobody ever highlights this. So, in a country where the basics are not right, we talk of advanced concepts of globalisation and six sigma! Because this is what the Americans talk about today. What we forget is that they talk about these things today because they have done well to give their people purchasing power as well as a functional legal system. China has this and so does Japan.

Of course till the macro changes take place, which often is outside the scope of a simple manager; he has to lead by example. In India itself I know of people as well as organisations which set ethical standards of behaviour. The *Tatas* as well as the *Hindustan Levers* are a benchmark for such standards. The fact is it's only difficult to be ethical (for example to say no to paying bribes) the first time around, the second time it becomes easier and the third time it becomes the way of life. Let there be corruption around but it is possible to strike an exceedingly ethical balance in life. This way you lead by example and the six people working under you or looking up to you start doing the same. It then becomes the way of life for 36 more and then for 216 more...

The idea that I recommend strongly at a very individual level is to set examples, instead of giving up. It's important to realise that even a paying a bribe of Rs. 100 to the traffic police is a non-patriotic and corrupt act. It's more important to realise that people who keep jumping over the line of integrity every now and then (fighting the acts as one-off instances) are the people who one day fail to locate the very existence of the line of integrity itself. I feel if one keeps jumping around the line of integrity, one day the line becomes so blurred that it practically ceases to exist... and that is scary for that reaches to the rule of the demon.

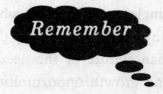 *Remember* That's what creates what we see today: "DEMONOCRACY" Instead of "DEMOCRACY".

Micro Aspects of "Theory 'i' Management"

At a micro level, Indian leaders have to necessarily increase the element of human touch in their organisations. They need to realise the importance of the first and second principles of theory 'i' management. Indians attach a high degree of importance to long-term relationship possibilities coupled up with growth opportunities. The fact is that we actually do not mind letting go of more materialistic pursuits for the sake of emotions (long-term relationships) and individual growth.

Top journalists who joined the *Observer* group for bigger packages left the company in no time the moment they saw their growth opportunities as journalists and individuals totally cramped. No wonder the newspaper itself did not last. By virtue of some of my personal interactions with multinational organisations which believe in bringing in expatriate managing directors, I can guarantee that nothing could be more counter-productive in a country like India. **The moment top people realise that growth stops at a point, they start feeling demotivated.**

Moreover I have not met a single expatriate MD who has ever been able to make any sense to me. They do not understand Indians, Indian culture or the needs for long-term relationship and growth opportunities that Indians crave for. Coupled with the feeling that a good proportion of these guys even sound racist (at least the employees feel so and have indicated the same to me) it makes a totally counter-productive idea.

India is a land of brilliance and capabilities. If a company cannot find a capable Indian to lead it, it has no business to be in India. The worst part is that the people deputed to India are very often the least capable ones. At least, that's what I found after interacting with them. Not only do I find them incapable of understanding Indians, I even find them handicapped when it comes to business sense. I am almost sure most of the companies like *Nestle*, *LG*, etc. with expatriates at top are being run by the brilliance of the Indian employees and not their MDs. The only thing that I, personally, find the expatriates capable of contributing to is demotivation! I strongly believe that if these companies are doing less than their potential it must be due to this policy of having a foreigner at the top who has less understanding of the Indian people and conditions. In India no organisation can think of achieving its full potential without taking care of its people in terms of emotions and growth opportunities.

To achieve this, like the Japanese, Indians too need to come out with people-centric policies that are effective—policies that help you remain committed to your people even in times of recession (that's the only way you can expect your people to remain committed to you).

Commitment is always a two-way process and organisations which expect their people to be committed without they being committed to their people need to restructure their philosophies. In India, more than corporate restructuring what is required is "Brain and Thinking Process Restructuring" at the top level. In my organisation the bonus and incentives make more than 60% of the salaries. Apart from my firm I just know of *Sahara* as another company where the basic salary is often as low as 10%. *Sahara* is an example of a company based in UP (many top CEOs I know of swear UP is the last place they want to do business in due to union/mafia problems) which has had no union problems inspite of having a large manpower base. Subroto Roy, is not the MD of the company... He is the "managing worker" and all the workers have stake in the company. Thus, people at *Sahara* feel proud to belong and work at *Sahara* collectively and individually, and in the morning they wish each other "Good Sahara". Of course when it comes to people-centric practices one cannot forget the name of the leader who is today a benchmark for all others. Yes, I am talking about Narayan Murthy of *Infosys*. He leads from the front and people are the core of his business. Though these leadership styles fulfil the first two principles of "theory 'i' management", yet, human touch and long-term relationships should not result into endless job security (as was done successfully in Japan) since, then, the elements of complacency are bound to creep in. This is so since culturally the Japanese have always been aggressive unlike Indians who, our experience says, grab and enjoy the first opportunity to become complacent.

THEORY 'i' MANAGEMENT
PERFORMANCE SAND DUNE
JOB SECURITY VS PERFORMANCE

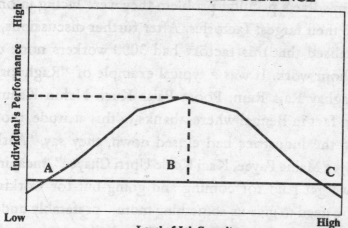

Situation	Level of Job Security	Characteristics Displayed by the Individual	Individual's Performance	Functional Viability
A	Low or None	THE ASS Job Hopper, Erratic, Demotivated, Irritable	Low	Creative turned Non-committed DYSFUNCTIONAL
B	Optimal	THE HORSE On his toes, Committed, Creative, Responsible, Result-oriented	High	FUNCTIONAL FUNCTIONAL FUNCTIONAL
C	High	THE COW Complacent, Lethargic, Non-competitive, Apathetic	Low	Creative-turned Vegetable DYSFUNCTIONAL

FIGURE - I

WHOM DO YOU PREFER ? THE ASS, THE COW OR THE HORSE ?

_____ ARINDAM CHAUDHURI _____

I went to take one of my initial workshops in a company owned by one of India's top three business houses. At the end of the workshop, the GM-HR seemed very impressed and asked me if I could help him solve a peculiar problem they were facing in one of their largest factories. After further discussions, I realised that this factory had 3000 workers none of whom work. It was a typical example of "Raghupati Raghav Raja Ram, Poora Paisa Kuch Nahin Kaam" (in fact in Bengal where, thanks to this attitude, most of the industries had closed down, they say, "Aashi Jayee Maina Payee, Kaaj Korle Uprri Chayee", meaning "we get paid for coming and going but for working you need to give us something more—preferably under the table"). But that's common in India.

What made this case unique was the fact that out here the managers had also formed a union and stopped working. The situation was such that when the top management required a file, they had to go and bribe these unionised middle-level managers to get the file out. YES!! I am talking about a private sector firm. This group sadly even today retains these values of lifetime employment and is full of lazy laggards who are its bane. Now I hear of a remarkable turnaround initiated by the young blood of the company working wonders for the same organisation.

I feel proud of this revival of one of our best and traditional organisations with a great history and principled past.

Another leading private television manufacturing firm had a similar problem. They were the leaders in the Indian market till the recent onslaught of foreign brands. Complacency had crept in. They had orders coming in from African countries and the company was not meeting deadlines. The CEO obviously was tense. When asked, the top managers would reply that they were working on a larger order from another country. The CEO realised that if they were not to meet these deadlines, small or big, these markets might be lost forever as the contracts could go to other competing firms. He wanted a change in the attitudes. He called for an attitude change workshop (thankfully, I was not the guy who was called. This case came to me much later) for his top 17 people. Between 2 to 5 p.m. the day before the workshop, it seems about 14 of them left for various emergency duties out of station. The next day there were just 3 people in the workshop and obviously it was called off! Later, upon being asked, these top people shouted back that when the company was small they were the people who slogged it out and now how dare anybody suggest that they needed a change in their attitudes. A typical Indian statement!

Even the management of this company has this thing about lifetime employment. The employees too are very well aware that their jobs are totally secure, so this attitude.

It's criminal to allow your workers to remain unproductive. Keep them unproductive and give them endless job security and they will turn into spineless parasites and suck your company dry.

Thus, to make Indians productive, job security levels would play a crucial role (typically the choice is explained in the **Performance Sand dune:** Figure I). I believe the levels of job security in the Indian context can affect productivity levels. Indians with high job security tend to become complacent while too much job insecurity can throw an averagely creative brain into a spin. However, it varies from person to person and their levels of maturity. The choice is between (a) giving endless job security to your people like the PSUs or the private companies I just mentioned and turning them into **Sleepy Cows** (b) giving total insecurity to your people and turn them into **Scared Asses** or (c) putting some efforts and fine tuning the ideal level of job security with a human touch and turning your people into **Galloping Horses**.

LEADING THE CHANGE

Of course the debate on how to reach a balanced level of job security can go on endlessly. That is why we call management an art. A good leader knows how to identify the correct level of job insecurity and match it up with the right amount of human touch. This is where leadership styles play a big role. Indian leaders could do well, perhaps, by implementing Theory

> **Very few countries can boast of having leadership traits and theories ingrained in their culture like the Indians can.**

'i' Management with the help of Indian leadership techniques which are explained beautifully in some of our epics like "The Gita" and the Saam, Daam, Dand, Bhed (I have given a little touch of modernity to the concept of Bhed, though. In my theory I have related Bhed with aspects of ruling/leading by dividing and delegating responsibilities) philosophy, etc. which talk about flexible styles of handling people based upon situations and backgrounds (this I have explained in my **"Leadership Success Multiplier" model: figure II**). Very few countries can boast of having leadership traits and theories ingrained in their culture like the Indians can.

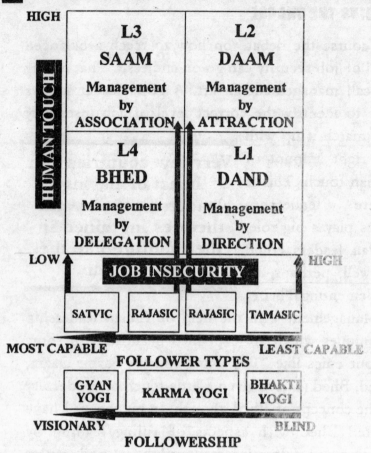

LEADERSHIP SUCCESS MULTIPLIER

FIGURE - II

TO EACH ACCORDING TO HIS NEED: THE INDIAN WAY

— Arindam Chaudhuri —

If we take a look into the Gita then we see that Lord Krishna talks about *Three Types* of people; The *Tamas*, The *Rajas* and The *Satwas*. Tamas are the people who are least capable and also less in number. Satwas are the people who are most mature and capable and also less in number. While Rajas are the majority. They are like most of us: intelligent, capable and ready to work but looking for the right returns. By combining the leadership principles of Saam, Daam, Dand and Bhed (Saam means equality; Daam means price; Dand means punishment; and Bhed means division), with different types of people of Gita, we can device a leadership strategy which suits each category of people.

Again, in order to explain things better, my model has divided Rajas into two categories. Category 1 comprising of Rajas with lesser capabilities, and category 2 comprising of Rajas who are more capable. A look now at figure II would tell you how to lead whom. Dand is for those who display lack of capabilities and responsibility on the job. They need **Leadership by Direction** in order to develop the right attitude. Those who become more mature (over time or naturally) require **Leadership by Seduction**. Incentives/Daam works for them. They are not the most responsible of people, therefore job insecurity still needs to be around; but if they work well human touch should be displayed.

As they become more mature, a time comes when job insecurity levels can be decreased and leadership can be by associating (**Leadership by Association**) them in the decision-making process. Trying to incentivise everything with this group of people can backfire, for they are looking for recognition. Those who are most mature/Satviks would be most productive with the least job insecurity, and perhaps even without any extra display of human concern. They need to be left alone and trusted completely. **Leadership by Delegation** works wonders with them (for most effective use and descriptive details of these four styles one should refer to (Figures III, IV, V & VI).

Now that I put the theory on pen and paper I realise that even I have grown up in its shadows.

As a kid I was particularly enthralled and at the same time jealous of the stove inside the kitchen. My mother would take utmost care of me. The only time she was not with me was when she was performing her kitchen chores. Needless to say the first opportunity I got as I began to crawl I entered the kitchen and tried to touch the beautiful red yellow flower on the burning stove. My mother's shriek and a slap, later I realised I better be careful. I did not understand why it hurt but I knew my mom was telling me something and I better not disobey. No sweat; anyway life was good and I was happy as a lark. If the kitchen was a no-entry zone the living room was my kingdom. All guests and relatives who would come to our house would play with me. The guest of honour would always be me as they lifted, cajoled, played and praised me. All was well until one day I answered the call of nature as and when it came in the playing room right there on the very expensive carpet. Holding me by my ear my mom led me to the bathroom and dumped me on the potty. I was told never again to do it anywhere else. Next morning almost before I got up I realised that my mother had put me on the potty. She seemed to have no concern about my feelings and my wants. And I call it the first style of leadership: **Leadership by Direction.**

I grew up to go to school. Those were the best days of my life with the exception of a subject called Hindi. None of the red marks in all my report cards, mocking smiles of my classmates and the regular scolding by my parents could propel me into securing decent marks in that subject. However, much to everybody's relief, what did the trick was my father's promise to buy me a cricket bat if I cleared my Hindi paper in the board exam. The shopkeeper may have physically sold the bat to a customer but the actual selling was done by my father. He got me attracted to the idea of finally being able to dethrone Vijay (the cricket kit belonged to him) and appoint myself as the new captain of the cricket team. I call it the second style of leadership: **Leadership by Seduction.**

Few years later with dreams unlimited and three appointment letters up my sleeve, I went to my father to help me make the right career decision. This time however there was no threat on me to do something he wanted nor was there a carrot hanging in front of me to pick one particular offer. Rather, he sat down with me and discussed the pros and cons of each offer. Together we went to a few counsellors, mentors, relatives in fairly high positions, analysed and came to a conclusion. He however left the final decision to me. He was participating in a historic moment of my life showing me the way and yet letting me decide. This is what I call third style of leadership: **Leadership by Association.**

A few years later was another decision time. I had worked hard and set up a fast-growing consulting firm and the day had come for me to start thinking of opening global branches. It meant more work and less time for home. This also meant lot of travelling. However, this time my father never made the decision any easier for me. He asked to be let alone happy in the company of his grandchild and delegating the task to me fully suggesting that any decision I took would be welcome by him. It was surprising that he did not even want to discuss it with me. I decided totally on my own. This is what I call the fourth and the final style of Leadership: **Leadership by Delegation.**

Thus, the four situation styles varied with my maturity level. My mother never tried reasoning with me as to how hazardous the fire could be, nor did she try to participate in a discussion with me, nor try to explain the fact that the beautiful rug was a gift by my father to her during their honeymoon. I was extremely immature and only the style of leadership by direction could have worked on me then—the slap. She knew leadership by direction was the only alternative with the immature me. When my dad lured me into studying hard he knew that it was that age when children run away from homes if parents are too directive. Thus, he used leadership by seduction.

When I got a job the style changed to leadership by association and in the later stages it became leadership by delegation, since in the later stages of life he realised that my abilities had also increased and I did not need directive or attractive styles. **Parents are seen often to be great managers. They love their children too much to give them anything but the** best. That's why the best theory of leadership is the "true love theory of leadership".

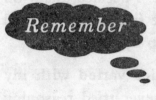

The moral of the story is that if you love your subordinates as much as parents love their children, these leadership instincts would come automatically to you like it comes to parents.

The idea is that a true leader has to understand that he cannot have a single style of leadership working effectively on everybody. Thus, he needs to constantly keep changing his styles to suit the situation depending upon the ability and maturity level of his people. And situations can differ and be more complex.

The same Sachin Tendulkar who would look like the most mature person on the cricket field might be the most immature person when it comes to playing piano and his levels of maturity might differ when he is dealing with his parents or with his wife. To make him play piano better, we might need to use leadership by direction whereas to make him excel as a cricketer the right style would be leadership by delegation. To make him pose as a model for an advertisement campaign might require leadership by seduction. So, the same style will not work even with the same person all the time because situation defines leadership.

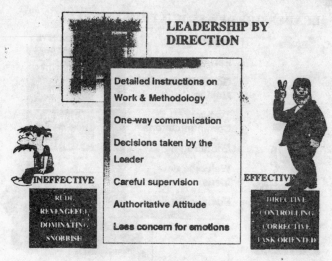

LEADERSHIP BY DIRECTION

Detailed Instructions on Work & Methodology

One-way communication

Decisions taken by the Leader

Careful supervision

Authoritative Attitude

Less concern for emotions

INEFFECTIVE

RUDE
REVENGEFUL
DOMINATING
SNOBBISH

EFFECTIVE

DIRECTIVE
CONTROLLING
CORRECTIVE
TASK ORIENTED

FIGURE - III

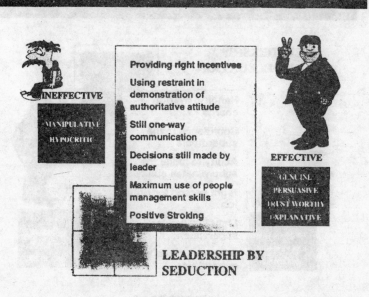

INEFFECTIVE

MANIPULATIVE
HYPOCRITIC

Providing right incentives

Using restraint in demonstration of authoritative attitude

Still one-way communication

Decisions still made by leader

Maximum use of people management skills

Positive Stroking

EFFECTIVE

GENUINE
PERSUASIVE
TRUSTWORTHY
EXPLANATIVE

LEADERSHIP BY SEDUCTION

FIGURE - IV

LEADERSHIP BY ASSOCIATION

- Initiating
- Participative
- Group Decision Making
- Two-way Communications
- Encouraging
- Welcome new Ideas
- Positive Stroking

EFFECTIVE

INVOLVING
ASSOCIATIVE
LEADING BY EXAMPLE
CHARISMATIC
EMPOWERING
ETHICAL
VISIONARY

INEFFECTIVE

UNINVOLVED
SUPERFICIAL

FIGURE - V

LEADERSHIP BY DELEGATION

- Handing over of charge
- Confidence in the subordinate
- Ability to judge the subordinates ability
- Right person for right job
- Light but regular supervision
- Decisions made by subordinate

INEFFECTIVE

LACK OF TRUST
UNINVOLVED
UNATTACHED
AVOIDING

EFFECTIVE

TRUSTING
ASSESSIVE
INTUITIVE
CONFIDENT

FIGURE - VI

THE MANAGERIAL PERSPECTIVE TO LEADERSHIP SUCCESS MULTIPLIER MODEL

A manager, early in the morning, may be confronted by immature labourers trying to make a wooden partition and a strict approach could do wonders; but by afternoon when he meets his sales team he might find leadership by seduction a better style. With his strategic planners, leadership by association could work wonders, while his R&D people might hate to sit down and discuss with him the medicine on which they are doing a research. These guys might be most motivated with leadership by delegation. The same man during the course of the same day might need to use different styles of leadership... and only then can he be a successful leader. I can assure you it would come automatically if you love your subordinates and are committed to them sincerely.

Frederick Herzberg in a path-breaking article titled *One more time: How do you motivate employees?*, way back in 1967, showed how KITA—the externally imposed attempt by management to motivate employees was a total failure. However, in my leadership success multiplier model, one would have observed that KITA definitely serves the purpose of leadership very well, at least in about 50% of the situations.

As an immature kid one of the best ways my parents could have taught me a few very important things like not putting my hand inside the stove etc. was done best with the help of a **KITA** (**Kick In The Rearside**). KITA may sound inelegant and taboo in organisations; however a negative psychological KITA could be a very effective way of dealing with people who are less mature. In fact that is exactly how I started using the potty. The fear of a scolding made me get up everyday in the morning and go towards it mechanically. One could not have explained to me the advantages of this good habit at that age! Actually, this negative psychological **Kick In The Backside** approach is one of the ways of implementing leadership by direction! Of course we don't call it motivation since in this case the individual had no urge to do the activity and it was forced on him.

The other way of implementing KITA is the positive psychological kick in the pants. When I tell somebody do this for me and in turn I give him a reward as in the earlier example, when my dad lured me into studying hard by offering me a cricket bat in return; it was an example of positive psychological KITA. Even in this case I have no urge to study hard on my own, I am falling for the bait. Motivation is of course when there is no external generator being used. It is a situation where the person has an internal generator urging him to put efforts (high levels at that) in order to achieve results. But this positive psychological KITA (which even Herzberg described as getting seduced) did improve my board examination results

[
**The man
who gets the most
satisfactory
results is not only
the man with the
most brilliant
sigle mind,
but rather the
man who can
best coordinate
the brains
and talents
of his associates.**
]

and today I don't feel ashamed to tell people about the same. So, in a way positive psychological Kick In The Pants is one of the ways of effective leadership by seduction.

Thus, leadership by direction and leadership by seduction are two ways of KITA that can be effectively used to make people achieve results. While leadership by direction is a push strategy, leadership by seduction is a pull strategy.

To my surprise, whenever I start talking about management by direction, many top corporate leaders resent, while most of them find management by seduction a very effective strategy. All I have to say in this regard is that I couldn't agree more with Herzberg when he said "If negative KITA is rape, positive KITA is seduction and it is infinitely worse to be seduced than to be raped; the latter is an unfortunate occurrence while the former signifies that you were a party to your own downfall". In fact he goes on to say that "this is why positive KITA is so popular. It is a tradition; it is in the American way. The organisation does not have to kick you; you kick yourself". By telling you this, I want to say that one should not have problems in using management by direction in certain situations because it can be effective, and if this style is bad, the popular style of leadership by seduction could be termed worse!

The last two styles of leadership by association and leadership by delegation of course are the motivators.

These styles do create an internal generator inside the employees to perform better, since these styles deal with empowering the employee, giving him a sense of responsibility, achievement and recognition as well as growth and advancement. These two styles of leadership can be thus successful only if the above things take place in the form of job enrichment.

This is what "Leadership Success Multiplier" is all about. And this is what Lord Krishna was a master of.

Lord Krishna...

A man standing on one leg with the other crossed over it; a flute in his hand; long locks of hair and a mysterious look in his eyes. Every time I close my eyes and try to think of him, this is the picture that keeps coming back. The picture doesn't remind you of a dynamic corporate leader, nor does it remind you of a tough task master. Yet, he happens to be the greatest of all leaders that I can think of.

And as my professor **Dr. N.R.Chatterjee** used to jokingly say "this man had two great qualities which leaders in general don't—he knew how to dance and how to make others dance!". Everytime invariably, whatever the situation, this man used to be a winner. The man I talk about is none other than the most loved of the Hindu Gods, a God viewed as a teacher, a God who did not only believe in war but a God of love who gives those who worship Him a gift of grace. A loving God could be found here and there in the old Vedic hymns of the Aryans, but this God, Lord Krishna, brought about a new focus for he offered salvation without the need for ritual sacrifices* thereby posing a challenge to Hindu priests. His sayings are contained in Bhagvad Gita (the Lord's song), which has become Hinduism's most popular scripture and is read by many for daily reference. It is a work that even Mahatma Gandhi described as an infallible guide to conduct. Sadly modern times have seen many more people just tie it up with a red cloth and keep it in their puja room, hardly ever bothering to read it. One of my professors used to keep his Gita in the bathroom instead of the puja room. He used to say, this way one gets at least a guaranteed concentrated reading time of about 15 minutes daily!

Lord Krishna knew how to be effective. He knew when to use management by direction with Arjun (Bhagvad Gita!!) and when to delegate him the complete responsibility (during the war). He knew exactly how to make even Yudhishtir mislead Dronacharya and he knew exactly how to handle the other extreme ideas of Duryodhan. Like a specialist

---

*Krishna said, "Give me your heart. Love me and worship me always. Bow to me only, and you will find me. This I promise." (Bhagvad Gita, 1:41)

conductor he orchestrated the whole war of Mahabharat, from managing Bhishma's temper to Bhim's lack of intelligence, from managing the illusion of the sun being still there to managing the end of Karna, from managing the guile of Shakuni to managing the anger of Dhritrashtra. He did it all with amazing smoothness. When it was required he used Dand/Leadership by Direction/negative psychological KITA to manage someone like Shishupal. When Gandhari called upon Duryodhan and there was a fear that he might become immortal, Lord Krishna used his intelligence through leadership by seduction and saw to it that it was not to be. While Lord Ram is known for his efficient

> **"this man had two great qualities which leaders in general don't—he knew how to dance and how to make others dance!"**

leadership, Lord Krishna is known for his effective leadership. One can bet that neither a Manthara would have made Lord Krishna (had he been in Lord Ram's place) leave his kingdom nor a Dhobi would have made him ask his wife to go through Agniparikshas.

My professor, Mr. Chatterjee, was once called upon by one of his client companies for an HR consulting assignment. The shop floor workers were not as effective as the management would want them to be. Mr. Chatterjee during his visit to the shop floor came to a conclusion that probably because the floor supervisor who was a tall hefty jat used a lot of foul language and started the day by abusing the workers seven generations was not creating a very conducive work culture in the organisation. He suggested to the management to replace this supervisor with one sober-looking Bengali chap who was armed with an MBA degree. The management made the changes but within two months quickly sent an S.O.S to Mr. Chatterjee stating that the situation on the contrary had only deteriorated further.

Undertaking a focus-group interview, Mr. Chatterjee learnt from the floor workers that "the new supervisor is so meek that he almost resembles a girl and addresses us as comrades. If we are all comrades and equal brothers then why does he get a higher salary than us. Let him also share his salary with us. He gets a higher salary only because he is required to get work done out of us. The earlier supervisor was a real 'mard' (masculine) and knew exactly how to get work done out of us and take decisions. True that he used a lot of slang but nevertheless he was effective. Please ask the management to bring back the enthusiasm, the excitement and the raw laughter that prevailed earlier". While telling this example to me,

THE FOLLOWERSHIP FACILITATOR

Type of worker/ subordinate	Ideal follower-ship style	Key characteristics
Immature, Low in ability and responsibility (found in less numbers)	**BHAKTIYOGIS** Blind/faithful/unquestioning	Should display full faith in the leader, and take regular guidance from him. Should not question the ability of the leader/top management. Should have an urge to learn and grow in order to enter the next level of worker category.
Mature, able and responsible (majority of the people fall in this category).	**KARMYOGIS** Work is worship oriented.	Should act responsibly and take guidance from the leaders whenever required. They should guide their subordinates to achieve better results. Should display leadership abilities since they are the leaders or the future leaders
Extremely mature and very high in ability (the rare breed).	**GYANYOGIS** Visionary, change agents.	Should work independently in order to achieve best results. Should be the change agents wherever they go. They should be given respect by the top management or made partners in progress.

FIGURE - VII

Prof. Chatterjee stated that he had learnt a valuable lesson on situational leadership more than all books put together on the topic.

In fact, all management books as well as management gurus talk about leadership, but nobody ever talks about **Followership**; however, the Gita does (this is where essentially theory 'i' leadership would differ from a model like that of Hersey & Blanchard). When the Tamas come to him in order to reach God (i.e. Him), Lord Krishna advised them to have blind faith that He exists and he says that this blind faith would lead them to God. Thus, he calls them the **Bhaktiyogis** (the faithfuls).

On the other hand when the other extreme kind of people, the Satwas, come to him he advises them to deny the existence of God and go in search of truth. And he says that this visionary journey would help them actually discover that he exists. Thus, he calls them the **Gyanyogis** (the visionaries). When the more common lot the Rajas approach him he tells them to keep on doing their work in a devoted manner to reach him. For them work should

> So, he talks about followership from blind to work oriented to visionary as the key to success.

be worship and he calls them **Karmayogis** (the work oriented). By teaching these principles of followership, Lord Krishna was able to manage them so successfully.

One might argue that while Lord Krishna wanted them to do their work without bothering about results (*ma phaleshu kadachana*)... this book is about working with the end in mind (count your chickens before they hatch). For that I would like to clarify that in the first chapter itself, I said that success is about giving your best effort on what you believe in; it is not about how much you earn from it or whether you have actually achieved what you set out for. Success for me is about having a clear goal in mind, which has achievable possibilities and for which you have put in your best efforts.

Remember

Followership can be of three types: faithful/blind, work oriented and visionary. And teaching principles of followership to your subordinates is the key to success.

Coming back to followership I must say that it is extremely sad that most of the Indian organisations don't adhere to it. The top level people who are supposed to be visionary (Gyanyogis) are converted into Bhaktiyogis, thanks to the bureaucratic machinery and red-tapism existing in our system. A fourth class under-secretary, thanks to the system, has the power to sign a document for which he has the audacity to make a Rahul Bajaj wait outside his office for four hours! The exit policies and politically motivated union activities have made the bottom level people the Gyanyogis (or so it seems, looking at the way endless number of trade unions have brought work to a halt) without proper education or experience. These people today through union activities have been instrumental in ruining corporate India.

Perhaps, the only example which comes to my mind as an immediate exception is that of the army. Knowingly or by default, the army focuses on followership. Thus, the bottom-level soldier blindly follows orders without asking questions while the middle-level captains carry on their work religiously and top-level generals strategise. I do strongly think that focus should also be put into aspects of followership in organisations as well. By implementing the followership facilitator model (figure VII) the roles would be better defined and work would be smoother.

I, thus, strongly feel that followership is as important as leadership, since leadership success depends upon how well the followers are trained, disciplined and explained their future career path. To my mind one of the greatest learnings from the Gita would be followership training. We have personally been giving it in a couple of public sector giants, and it works. People can be easily explained their optimal role in an organisation and made to be productive and cooperative. It is highly important that they are told their career path and the appraisal is totally transparent. Most importantly they should know that the whole process is to help them mature up to the visionary level. The leader also has to facilitate the followers mature from one level to another. The identification of the follower category is also extremely important. Attempts to make a blind follower out of a man (who might be looking for self-actualization needs) capable of making independent decisions and strategise are futile.

I know of several cases of top thinkers, researchers and journalists who left their highly paid jobs for less paid ones, only because they were treated as visionaries and given the due freedom. Understanding the people working for you and making them understand your priorities is the only way you can have true subordination of individual interests into group interests. Experience would show that till we have this, organisations can never work productively and optimally. Of course the implementation of all these models would differ from situation to situation. The philosophy should not.

Mahatma Gandhi...

In a different age another great leader, a true devout of Lord Ram (Hey Ram!), actually put the learnings from Lord Krishna to practice to lead a nation from the shackles of the British Raj towards independence—Mahatma Gandhi. He is said to have had the habit of reading the Gita regularly. Having been ruled for so many years by one foreign power or the other, the Indian populace had been accustomed and acclimatized to exploitation. There were a few raised voices here and there, a few bombs hurled around but never did a revolt of the types of 1857 end up having a nationwide impact like it happened all over the world viz. France, Scotland, USA, Russia, China, etc. India was a different nation which needed "Lord Krishna's Leadership".

What succeeded everywhere else failed in India and what was never tried anywhere else succeeded with the Indians. The success of this non-violent revolution is perhaps, thus, the biggest lesson for the Indian managers. It should make them realise the importance of coming out with unique management concepts for Indians... because it seems we are actually an unique combination of values, cultures and lethargy (if I am permitted to use this word!).

A brave man Netaji Subhash Chandra Bose became the President of the Indian National Congress defeating Gandhiji's own candidate. But did he succeed? He came up with a war cry "Give me blood and I will give you freedom". He walked forward a few steps and turned to look back to realise that nobody was following him. To fight India's Independence, Netaji had to go to Burma and Japan to collect war veterans and freedom fighters. No one in India wanted Independence that badly or rather as a nation we refused to give blood, so what it was for the country's Independence. The Indians historically and culturally would never do it (again due to the laid-back and complacent attitude). Like the Cow (as I mentioned earlier) whom we worship, we would not mind sitting in the middle of a busy four-lane, high-speed road with traffic zooming past... global changes sweeping the way things work... we can remain unfazed and unmoved, for we wait for things to happen instead of making them happen.

Gandhi came up with a suitable alternative. He understood the Indian psyche well. So he asked them to march with him. A wonderful hassle-free method to get Independence and so every Indian marched, walked with Gandhi to the doorsteps of an Independent India.

The world over bloody revolutions have led to independence but we attained it through **"ahimsa (non-violence movement)"**. Whether it was more by default than choice could be another story. (If Mike Tyson were to challenge me for a boxing bout I would tell him straight that I belonged to the land of Gandhi, and ahimsa is what I believed in!).

Gandhi not only understood the Indians well but had also analysed the Britishers correctly.

He knew that by and large the Britishers were law-abiding and would only retort to brutality if law was broken, and peaceful and non-violent marching broke no laws. I dread to imagine as to what would have happened to Gandhi if it had been Hitler's regime.

Mahatma Gandhi's example to me is a perfect case of adopting styles to suit the culture. The country today stands divided on whether what he did was good or bad... I just know one thing. There was never a leader before him or never one after him who could unite us all and bring us out in the streets to demand for what was rightfully ours. To me he is the greatest leader our land has ever seen. And to me it is "Theory 'i' Management" at its practical best—productively and intelligently utilizing whatever the resource you are endowed with.

On a lighter note it reminds me of two instances which I will never forget. They both unfortunately took place during the gory riots of 1984. Sikhs were being ruthlessly massacred and they were striking back. Our locality held a meeting to discuss the issues relating to local security during the time of the riots. Many ideas came up including one of organizing security groups with the help of the young members of the families by rotation. No conclusion seemed to be feasible—till somebody said we should all go back and remain alert inside our homes! And then there was consensus.

Fed up of no protests, somebody the next day called for a protest gathering at India Gate in order to voice the disgust against the riots. I pity him. He forgot that this was not USA, Russia or China where people come out on the streets to demand their rights. In Russia and China, people came to the streets inspite of the fear of ruthless, cruel and brutal treatment, as brutal as what happened in Tianmann Squares, whereas in India the maximum fear is of tear gas or water spray and yet to get people together we actually have to pay them.

Well, as expected, the protest never took place. What is interesting is that the very next day an intelligent man (a modern day micro version of Gandhi) called for a different kind of protest. He said that to protest against the riots we should all switch off our lights at 7 o'clock that evening and for five minutes, in the darkness of night, bang our utensils with spoons for five minutes. Interestingly, this was a big success bigger than any protest.

What I am trying to say basically is **we need to remove the dichotomy existing in our system,** where, on one hand, we keep harping about our culture and, on the other hand, we overlook this aspect completely when it comes to managing our people. We have to admit and realise that Indians are different. We have our positives and negatives. The idea is to utilize the positives and manage the negatives in order to succeed.

We have a strong culture, with tolerance and peaceful coexistence as our main forte. Rabindranath Tagore described India as a melting pot of all cultures and religions. Religions like Bahai which are banned in their country of origin still find place in India. How many countries can boast of people with respect for others and emotional bonding love for family? From these great traits emerge other aspects which may not be very conducive to easy handling. Yes, from our non-materialistic (or less materialistic) approach towards life emerges the "Chalta Hai" (complacent) attitude. Does it mean that we give up? No. It means that we require more careful and behaviour-centric management. Lord Krishna and Mahatma Gandhi have already shown how to make **galloping horses out of sleepy cows;** it's our turn now.

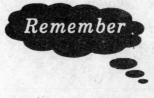

Yes! You can count your chickens before they hatch if you have the determination, the ability to work successfully with people and the flexible attitude of theory 'i' management with you!!

The performance sand dune, the leadership success multiplier as well as the followership facilitator might have Indian roots, but they are globally relevant tools for leading and managing people. Every country has different subcultures; every individual goes through various stages of life; and every person has different driving forces. They all need the right amount of job insecurity and human touch to be most productive. Making others productive and efficient is one of the most important aspects of organisational as well as national success. If we are to count our chickens before they hatch, we need to manage ourselves, our families and the people we work with effectively. In case we are able to do so, success would never elude us.

> *End note: Leadership is about having a flexible attitude. It is about matching your styles with the character traits of your subjects. It is also about guiding them on how to follow.*

IF YOU THINK YOU CAN YOU ARE RIGHT

The Indian Institute of Planning & Management

THE ROOTS

The year 1963; A dream; A proposal to Jawaharlal Nehru, the then Prime Minister of India to set up an Institute under the name of "Institute for Planning and Administration of National Economy"; A study tour of Europe & A man. The roots of an institute with a difference. An institute oriented towards the promotion of corporate growth, based on innovation and entrepreneurship in harmony with national economic planning objectives, aiming at a sustainable and ethically acceptable growth rate. This was conceptualised by an eminent professor of **IIM Bangalore, Dr. M.K.Chaudhuri.**

He travelled extensively throughout Europe to study similar institutions, and The Indian Institute of Planning and Management was formally registered in the year 1973.

TO KNOW MORE ABOUT IIPM AND

what happened since the year 1973...

what makes IIPM the most unique institute in the country...

what makes the maximum number of students join IIPM every year and remain crazy about it...

which paper Prof. Arindam Chaudhuri is teaching in the current semester...

log on to www.iipm.edu

PLANMAN
CONSULTING

DELHI · MUMBAI · BANGALORE · KOLKATA · TORONTO ·

It's alarming!

Hostile takeover threats, new excise policies,
BSE worries...
67% people report dwindling sexual desire due
to work uncertainities.

WELL, DOESN'T APPLY TO SMART PEOPLE WHO DO
BUSINESS WITH PLANMAN.

From charting an invigorating mission that drives to
designing processes for improved productivity; from
precision market & economy studies to smart product
& brand strategies; from quality training to searching
a CEO to hold the reigns, we do them all to help you
perform better. In business and in your LIFE.

Planman Consulting is today India's largest Multi-interest Indian
Multinational consulting firm. Our clients include more than 50%
of Fortune 100 companies.

Corporate India is being driven by Planman
Consulting. Don't be left behind.

log on to www.planmanconsulting.com or

The official jobsite of Planman:
GroovyJobs.com

News Editor, *NDTV, Vijay Trivedi* speaks... "An eye opener... some brilliant ideas, the best part was the experience shared by the participants and Mr. Arindam himself".

Mrs. Claude Bibeau Purohit, *Second Secretary, Canadian High Commission* speaks... "Recommendable... I can use in a practical way these tools of management and adapt them to various conditions."

Mr. Tehavdar Petkov, *Counsellor, Embassy of Bulgaria* speaks... "The speech of Prof. Chaudhuri was the best part... a well organised attempt to help participants to find focus at work."

Director, *HPCL, Mr. S.K. Kerr* speaks... "Very stimulating and very good live examples given. I discovered that "followership" training should be imparted and not only leadership training."

Director, *GAIL, Mr. S. Niyogi* speaks... "I liked the workshop... the best part was relating leadership styles with the message of Bhagwat Gita."

Chairman, *Enkay Group of Cos., Mr. Nanik Rupani* speaks... "Vedic way of corporate governance... very interesting."

Managing Director, *Gestetner India Ltd., Mr. K. Swetharanyan* speaks... "Good and new insight... new model on leadership."

CEO, *Jenson & Nicholson (I) Ltd., Mr. K. L. Batra* speaks... "An interesting way of looking at Indian management scenario... I must study "Gita" once more."

Executive Director, *Xerox Modicorp Ltd.* **Mrs. K.** *Bandhopadhyay* speaks... "The best part was Arindam Chaudhuri - his versatile and articulate style and passion for economics and management... Rejuvenating."

Managing Director, *Pepe Jeans, Chetan Shah* speaks... "Stimulating... I feel more refreshed and recharged from the workshop than my last vacation in Spain."

Executive Director, *ICI India Ltd., Mr. Daljit Singh* speaks... "A new perspective to management in India... thought provoking"

Sr. Director, *DOE, Ministry of Information Technology, S. Ramakrishnan* speaks... "Winning management styles can be learnt from Indian life and mythology itself... an opportunity to get a vision of important management ideas very effectively conveyed... an exercise required for every Sr. management person to rediscover what secret of success lie within him/her."

Managing Director, *Koshika Telecom Ltd., Mr. Jogesh Nayar* speaks... "Invigourating and motivating... an enlightning afternoon on a new dimension to leadership and management."

Executive Director, *Punj Lloyd, Mr. Subhash Jagota* speaks... "Rewarding experience and good learning... enthusiastic and forceful speaker with good contents."

Director, *Parke - Davis, Yugal Sikri* speaks... "A great speaker with great thoughts... simple, practical, implementable thoughts - all put together in an unassuming and touching style. Thankyou!!!"

Executive Director, *Hudco, Mr. P.M. Tripathy* speaks... "best way of exploring opportunities with applicability of concepts as required in organisations... Best was the way of presentation".

CEO, *Valvoline Cummins, Mr. Naveen Gupta* speaks... "Educative and participative... Practical, the best part was on personality reflection and the subtle issues involved in leadership traits"

Executive Director, *Baush & Lomb (I) Ltd., S. Tandon* speaks... "I discovered that leadership has to be a dynamic phenomenon... It was learning by participation".

COO, *Investmart (I) Ltd., S. Rengarajan* speaks... "The way Arindam smoothly moved from one topic to another and brought out the points with live examples was the best... very useful and interesting."

Director, *Frito-lay India, Mr. Samik Base* speaks... "A new perspective on leadership in the Indian context... a good learning experience."

Director - HR, *Bharti Telecom, Mr. G.K. Aggarwal* speaks... "Simply brilliant... an excellent talk - very simple but very powerful."

Managing Director, *Burr Brown India Ltd., Mr. D. Kar* speaks... "A forum for thought generation... new thoughts about the cultural aspects of management".

CEO, *Modi Korea Telecom, Mr. A.K. Chakarborty* speaks... "An opportunity to get enlightened on contemporary management thinking... An eye opener and a step in the right direction."

Associate Director, *Jones Lang Lasalle, Mr. Avnish Singh* speaks... "The workshop helped me discover that 'there are miles to go before I sleep i.e. loads of change to manage at my work place.'"

Managing Director, *Fulford (I) Ltd., K. D. Shah* speaks... "The best part was on the reasons why we are in a mess as a country."

Director, *Turner International India*, Mr. N. *Jhunjhunwala* speaks... "Excellent... an opportunity to access and understand totally from the Indian management context."

Sr. Director, *Hughes Escorts, Mr. R. Pandey* speaks... "It has helped me see a connection between Indian ethos and situational leadership."

Managing Director, *Fritz (I) Ltd., Mukesh Shah* speaks... "Excellent... all companies have common issues and by discussing among various MD's solutions can be found."

Managing Director, *MAP Auto Ltd., Yashpal Gupta* speaks... "If I were to make a film on the workshop the title would be Positive Mental Attitude".

Managing Director, *Technovinyl, K. C. Chandan* speaks... "True and realistic management workshop. It helped me realised the unlimited potential within me."

Managing Director, *Rama Compsys Ltd., R. Kumar* speaks... Some amazing concepts of Indian economy, the world market and leadership.

Chairman & Managing Director, *J. D. Institute of Fashion Technology, C. Dalal* speaks... "Best approach, simplified yet innovative – thanks to the "Guru". Absolute simplified version of "Gita" and "Gandhi" principles."

CEO & President, *Triune Projects Ltd. Mr. S.C.Mathur* speaks... "A wonderful experience... an excellent concept of management which can be easily put in practice".

CEO & Managing Director, *Topsgrup, Diwan Rahul Nanda* speaks... "Value for money... the best part was the unassuming attitude of Arindam – emotes very humanely and the theory of followership"

Head, OD&TQM, *Ranbaxy, Mr. R. Johree* speaks... "I discovered that leadership is still an area to explore, the best were the examples".

Chief Economist, *Hudco, Ms. Kiran Wadhwa* speaks... "Enlightening (Gyan Prapti)... the old school of participative management has very serious drawback. I could relate to my departmental functioning and benefited from the analysis".

V P, Citi Bank, *Atul Sharma,* speaks... "Management closer to Indian mindset... Wonderful co-relation between Hindu philosophy and modern management."

V P, Times Bank, *Milind B. Arge,* speaks... "I would describe the workshop as stimulating. The title of the workshop should be Towards a new being".

EVP, *McCann Erickson, Mr. Santosh Desai* speaks... "An Interesting perspective... very provocative in its intent... I am glad that someone is carrying the India Centric Theory Banner".

Jt. Managing Director, *Fena Ltd., Mr. Pradeep Jolly* speaks... "Interesting and useful... it was small, interactive and Prof. Chaudhuri's style was easy, communicative and lucid".

Jt. Managing Director, *Jayaswal Neco Ltd., Mr. Manoj Jayaswal* speaks... "I learnt how to set goals and achieve them... It should be called the "Krishna" workshop."

Director, *Cosco (I) Ltd. Neeraj Jain* speaks... It was cleansing up of the mind to provide new direction of thinking.

Director, *Royal Exports, Dhanraj Sawlani* speaks... "It can be best described as a school of winners."

Director, *Pie - Education, Mr. C.V.Kalyan Kumar* speaks... "An innovative, enlightening and a thought provoking workshop."

Head Corporate Affairs, *Duncans Industries Ltd. Mr. Sandeep Soni* speaks... "Guide to todays manager... I realised that there is lots to learn and improve".

EVP, *Ingersoll-Rand (I) Ltd, M.H.Gandhi* speaks... "A lovely experience... Zeroing on the essentials rather than be distorted by other things... most enlightening and wonderful experience."

Sr. V P, Jindal Iron & Steel, *R.P.Nangalia,* speaks... "Educative. The best part was the company of Mr. Arindam Chaudhuri and the concept of Theory 'I' Management."

Sr. V P, Global Trust Bank, *K.V.Ramesh,* speaks... "Thought provoking and enlightening... Best part was the comparison of leadership qualities of US, Japan, India and China."

VP, *Forbes Gokak, Ms. S. Kalra* speaks... "Had I not attended the workshop I would have missed the opportunity to attend Arindam Chaudhuri workshop 'live'... interesting and different".

General Manager, O&M, *Ms. Ritu Abrol,* speaks... "Healthy interaction woven together by the magnetic style of Arindam Chaudhuri..."

Sr. VP, Percept, *Mr. R. Ravi,* speaks... "Some valuable inputs... it helped me look at me once again."

Sr. Editor, Sahara TV, *Mr. Ashoke Aggarwal,* speaks... "An opportunity of a life time - a window for internal and external management introspection... treasure trove."

Finance Controller, Kopran, *Mr. Varun Sharda,* speaks... "One of the best opportunity (to learn)... can make me a good leader"

VP, *LNJ Bhilwara Group, N.K.Jain* speaks... "I am **delighted** to learn about the leadership concepts... It was **excellent** and mind opening."

VP, SABe TV, *Dr. Mala Kapadia,* speaks... "GOOD ! There are people who still believe in Indian theories of management..."

VP, *Gulf Oil, R. Vankataraman* speaks... "Very informative and educative."

Sr. General Manager, Godfrey Philips, *Mr. S. S. Kar,* speaks... "I realised that Indian management styles have all the ingredients of modern management... good learning"

AVP, Elf Lubricants, *Mr. Sanjoy K. Guha,* speaks... "Indian concept of management... we may have been practicing unknowingly, but now would be able to use effectively."

Head - IT, L&T, *Mr. P. Roy,* speaks... "I realise how important Prof. Chaudhuri is in today's context & the relevance of theory 'i' management... the best were the examples quoted with Prof. Chaudhuri's down to earth and witty style."

Regional - Head, Tata Infomedia, *Mr. Mandeep Singh,* speaks... "A good Indian context to the management styles... lot of serious corporate people have great concern for India and its progress."

Regional Business Head, BPL Ltd., *Mr. Sanjay Prasad,* speaks... "Thought provoking... I now realise why some of the countries and their people are successful and how cultures and management styles are in line (with each other)."

Head - Marketing, *Daewoo Motors, Mr. Debashish Gupta,* speaks... "Wonderful, Indian epic model developed by Prof. Chaudhuri. Feel proud to be an Indian. An entirely new experience! Great, I must say."

General Manager, Glaxo-Smithkline, *Mr. N.Narshimha Rao,* speaks... "The followership model in leadership was the best and the facilitation of Prof. Arindam and his knowledge added value."

Sr. Manager - Corporate Planning, *NTPC, P. Purkayastha* speaks... An exploratory journey... about the need to have a relook at our national economy in the backdrop of globalization and adopt the management style which fits the Indian culture... With the aim of bringing a future worth living.

Head - HRD, *Escorts Ltd., Mr. V.P.Sinha,* speaks... "A wonderful lecture... a new dimension to leadership styles."

VP, *Credit Lyonnais, Mr. Atul Sodhi,* speaks... "Excellent and eye opening... historic framework of Indian management."

VP, *K.C.Thappar Group, Mr. Ravi Sharma,* speaks... "Indian mantra" - suitable for the competitive world."

DGM, *E.I.Dupont, Mr. Vivek Bhargava,* speaks... "A great eye opener... a really good learning day."

Chief - HR & TQM, *Escotel, Mr. Rajan Dutta,* speaks... "Insightful and practical... the strength and weaknesses of Indians and Indian culture and the way to leverage performance in professional and personal settings."

Regional Manager, *Crompton Greaves Ltd., Col. H. B. Puri,* speaks... "There is a lot more to management and leadership than mere jargons... I learnt A HELLUVA LOT!!! The workshop was a real eye opener and will tell on my management skills in the company."

Kumar Kaushal, *Financial Express* speaks... "A rare peep into Prof. Arindam's incredible ability to demolish well established socio-economic doctrines... A stimulating blend of traditional, India - Centric and refreshing, innovative approaches to understanding leadership values."